PAINTING IN FRANCE
1895–1949

The CHANGING WORLD Series

Editor: Bernard Wall

ROUAULT   *Nude*

PAINTING IN FRANCE
1895—1949

BY

G. DI SAN LAZZARO

Translated by
BAPTISTA GILLIAT-SMITH and BERNARD WALL

LONDON
THE HARVILL PRESS

First published 1949
The Harvill Press Ltd
23 Lower Belgrave Street, London, S.W.1

Printed in Great Britain
At the Camelot Press, Southampton

Contents

List of Illustrations

vii

Foreword

IT isn't easy to describe anybody in a few words. I am not sure, to begin with, whether it would be more accurate to describe Gualtieri di San Lazzaro as an Italian or as a Parisian. If either word were used it would have to be given wide meaning. Fortunately, ever since the Middle Ages there have always been Italian Parisians.

The author of this book is still a relatively young man. He arrived in Paris in the twenties when he was very young indeed. With astonishing rapidity he integrated himself into the fertile life of the city—then in a great creative phase as regards the arts: he became intimate with most of the masters of the then contemporary movement in painting. That is how he got his background for what he writes on contemporary artists and their work. He isn't in any way a scholastic writer. One feels he has been through the experience of the artists he writes about, so to speak, and has accompanied them on their experiments. And so anecdotes about their personal lives are to be found side by side with descriptive passages. In the original text to which the translators have tried to be faithful one gets pieces of what I would like to call "plastic prose"—a kind of jotting which I feel interprets closely what the painters in question, too, are trying to reach in their medium. It is unusual for critics to write like this, but painters themselves often do. Anyway, San Lazzaro disclaims that his intuitive way of writing is criticism in the ordinary sense.

During the years between the two wars San Lazzaro played his part in the polemical life of the arts in Paris as editor and publisher as well as writer. In a book of memoirs which appeared this year in Italy he has described the ups and downs of his editor's life as well as the personalities he lived closest to: from Vollard to Picasso, from Zborowski to Severini.[1] He was successively in charge of *Les Chroniques du Jour*, an international literary periodical which helped to present Joyce, Dos Passos, Pilniak and Remizov to the French: *Chroniques du Jour*, an

---

[1] *Parigi era viva*, Garzanti, 1948.

art review of different scope in spite of the quasi-identity of title: and *XXme Siècle*. The latter was his most important enterprise apart from his writing, and had an English edition over which Zwemmer in London and Weyhe in New York collaborated. It stopped when the late war broke out.

San Lazzaro is the author of a number of prefaces and monographs: *Hommage à Charlot*, *Poésie* (with Joyce, Max Jacob, C. A. Cingria, Zborowski, and others), *Cézanne* (1935) and *Modigliani* (1948). He has written several volumes of reminiscences in Italian as well as the book here translated.

B. W.

Introduction

I HOPE no one who reads this book will look for a "history" of modern painting in France. My intention has only been to disentangle the most significant tendencies and to provide the main threads for those readers who are interested in the problems of modern art but have been put off by the "closed language" of critics which is more difficult to understand than the work it claims to explain.

But on the other hand this little guide to modern painting oughtn't to be considered an attempt at vulgarization. It is meant to be simply a friendly chat which has been inspired by love of art. I would like to thank in advance all those who have the patience to listen to what I have to say.

PARIS.   G. DI S. L.

No Masters and No Schools

I N December, 1895, Ambroise Vollard, a young dealer who had exhibited Forain with success two years earlier and was already looked on favourably by Pissarro and Degas, got up Paul Cézanne's first personal exhibition in his little gallery in the rue Lafitte, Paris.

1895 was therefore a date of capital importance in Cézanne's life. But, as Lionello Venturi has already pointed out with far more authority than mine, this date also stands as symbol of the new tendency in art which had begun to appear and grow during the previous years. It opened a new epoch. Art was freed from the tutelage of the State. The grand old Academy masters, laden with years and honours, who alone had had the power to judge whether an artist deserved a silver medal or mere praise, now became grotesque "officials", bereft of all prestige. With Vollard authority passed to the dealers. In the supreme interest of art, painting once again became a trade. Though doubtless he hadn't yet become the *fin lettré* of *Les Réincarnations de Père Ubu*, Ambroise Vollard was on his way to being the principal eyewitness of the greatest period of French painting. This period is European and consequently universal.

Degas and Renoir were beginning to get to know Vollard and to look up to him. Puvis de Chavannes welcomed him without interrupting his work. Count Isaac de Camondo, the arbiter of the collectors of the time, gave him his benevolent protection. And Vollard's excellent maidservant did not begrudge him her advice.

The young dealer had already gained some experience. He felt that the time was now ripe for an exhibition of Cézanne. Caillebotte's legacy to the Louvre had temporarily stirred up the anti-impressionist controversy. A few Fine Arts professors had threatened to hand in their resignations if the State accepted the collection. But the State had no way of ridding itself of the heirs who were firmly determined to respect the wishes of the deceased. Finally, in order to satisfy one lot of people without antagonising the other unduly, the State refused a good half of the collection—namely, eleven Pissarros, eight Monets, three Sisleys, three Cézannes, and one Manet. To-day they are worth about fifty million francs. But the professors did not resign.

In his *Cézanne*, Vollard devoted several pages to the exhibition. Though they fail to equal his *Déjeuner avec Rodin* in crudity, they are full of the mischievous laughter of little bronze satyrs on marble mantelpieces. "The agonising sight", the *Journal des Artistes* hastened to report, "of these atrocities in oil goes beyond the limits of legally authorised mystifications." Of the hundred or so canvasses exhibited, the following were the most noteworthy: *Leda and the Swan*, 1868; *The Feast*, 1868; a few self-portraits; *The Deserted House*, 1887; *The Forest of Chantilly*, 1888; *The Great Pine*, 1887; *Portrait of Madame Cézanne in the Hot-house*, 1891; *The Banks of the Marne*, 1888; *Bathers in Front of a Tent*, 1878; *Le Déjeuner sur l'Herbe*, 1878; *Madame Cézanne in a Green Hat*, 1888; *Le Jas de Bouffan*, 1888; *L'Estaque*, 1883. Nearly all the collectors, and even Vollard's maidservant, shared the opinion expressed in *Le Journal des Artistes*. "I am afraid, monsieur", his good servant kept on saying, "you will discredit yourself too much with the collectors if you keep that picture of 'nude gentlemen' in the window." "Fine advice I get from you!" grumbled Vollard. But for all that he was obliged to give in, to remove the painting of the "nude gentlemen" from the window, and other perverse anatomies from the walls.

When he turned round a picture facing the wall Auguste Pellerin discovered the *Leda* and bought it. In time Pellerin was to become the greatest collector of Cézanne's works, but his choice itself proves that in 1895 he was not yet ripe for the art of the painter of *Le Compotier*, *The Bathers in Front of a Tent*, *Le Déjeuner sur l'Herbe*, and many other pictures later to enrich his collection. The *Leda* is one of the pleasantest and easiest of his compositions, but probably just because of its vague pleasingness it misses being one of the most significant pictures in Cézanne's severe canon. It was Courbet's *La Femme et le Perroquet* which gave Cézanne, who in '68 was going through a period of romantic turmoil, the idea of painting *Pandarus'* honest wife with her Olympic lover, though all the time he pretended he didn't know the legend.

Another collector, Count de Camondo, whom I have already

mentioned, used to justify his purchase of *La Maison du Pendu*: "Well, yes, I have bought a picture which is not yet generally accepted, but I have a guarantee in the form of a letter from Claude Monet, written in his own handwriting, in which he gives me his word of honour that this picture is destined to become famous. If you call on me one day, I will show it you. I keep it in a little envelope glued on to the back of the canvas." And the ex-King of Serbia, Milan, as he was leaving the gallery with two water-colours under his arm, asked Vollard: "Why don't you advise that Cézanne of yours to paint charming little women instead?" Throughout those early battles for the new art Italy was represented too. The first really passionate collector of Cézanne's work was an Italian, Egisto Fabbri. And another great Cézanne collector, the American Charles Loeser, was Italian by domicile.

Lionello Venturi is right in saying that Cézanne's reputation dates from Vollard's exhibition. But Vollard was over-anxious not to mislead posterity about his contemporaries' taste, and only collected comic anecdotes about the exhibition. He almost forgot to add anything about the enthusiasm it aroused among the youngest and most intelligent of the artists.

Perhaps it was modesty that made Vollard refrain from attaching too much importance to Cézanne's first exhibition, since he himself played such an important part in it. But it is more likely that he saw nothing funny in the enthusiasm of the young artists and of one or two critics. Above all, he was always on the look-out for platitudes, puns, absurdities and all the ins and outs of the *petite histoire*. This mania caused him to transform the "nasty and uncouth" Degas into a great wit, almost a belated *boulevardier*. Vollard was such a great lover of anecdotes that he would stop at no pains, even in his old age, to add a few lines to his notebooks, and these he undoubtedly prized more highly than his folders, in spite of all the treasures the latter contained. When he wanted to explain to me how Renoir hit on the idea of painting him in the flamboyant costume of a bull-fighter (he had not yet published *Souvenirs d'un marchand de tableaux*, in which he gives the official version, so to speak, of that remote episode), he did not hesitate to haul his great Rabelaisian body—which after his sixtieth year made one think of a demiurge—up to my sixth-floor

3

flat, panting the while like a Minotaur grappling with Theseus in the labyrinths of Crete.[1]

Anyway, thanks to Vollard, the year 1895 is a date which stands out in the history of art. But to impress this on readers who are approaching the subject for the first time, I shall take the liberty granted to novelists and go back briefly to the origins of the art of our century.

For one step forward in some particular direction which they manage to force on society, revolutions take a hundred steps backwards in every other. To become emancipated from classical inspiration, art and literature had to wait until the nineteenth century. People in that century abandoned themselves to a philosophical *douceur de vivre*, and the few who outlived the *ancien régime* looked back to it with regret. The Revolution, which gave freedom to the people, denied it to artists. And the Empire was no more generous. The only freedom granted to artists was freedom to celebrate the Empire and to praise its heroic spirit. For the first of the modern dictators, like his pathetic imitators, concealed tyranny from the eyes of the people under the banner of heroism. So as to invest the imperial idea with some grandeur, David astutely evoked Rome—not the Rome from which the Emperor had summoned the Pope to place the imperial crown on his head, but the Rome of the Cæsars. Empires are fed on myths, and David took over the legends of Rome in which Greek mythology survived intact. Leonidas of Thermopylæ alternated with the oath of the Horatii. After David, Ingres celebrated Œdipus and the Sphinx and painted the apotheosis of Homer.

[1] Vollard delighted in posing for his favourite painters. Cézanne's portrait of him required more than a hundred sittings, but Renoir, though he worked more rapidly, after first painting him like Titian's antiquarian, Strada, with a statuette in his hands, then with a cat on his lap, finally told Vollard to order himself a suit of blue material, a blue with cold, metallic reflections. So Vollard set about trying to find such a colour, but in vain: he was never able to find the exact blue Renoir wanted. In the end, at Renoir's request, he brought back from Spain a flashing toreador outfit which he had been obliged to put on at the Customs, amidst a laughing crowd of onlookers, in order to prove to the officials that it was his own. When Renoir saw him appear dressed like this, he said to him: "That is how I want to paint you."

It was the ambition of Cézanne's dealer to be able to print "*Ambroise Vollard, éditeur*" on the cover of a book. Though he was not always fortunate in his choice of illustrators, it was he who obtained for book production the collaboration of the greatest French painters: Picasso, Degas, Odilon Redon, Rouault, Bonnard, Dufy and Chagall. And if it is true that it was also as a result of his instigations that Renoir, like Degas, decided to take up sculpture, this happy suggestion, coupled with his invaluable work as dealer and editor, should be taken into account in awarding him a place in history. The influence of *Vénus* and *La Grande Baigneuse* on modern plastic art was decisive. Degas used to say that one takes on too much responsibility if one leaves a work in bronze behind one—"that material for eternity". But a portion of this "eternity" is certainly deserved by Vollard. He was killed in a motor accident in 1939, when he was almost eighty.

4

But David accused Ingres of being a revolutionary, and Ingres, who had to defend himself, called himself the champion of the tradition of Raphael. But, true enough, Ingres freed art of one of the hundred chains which oppressed it. In their *Modern Painting*, Ozenfant and Jeanneret recognised that "a painting by Ingres is a perfectly homogeneous symphony in which the subject only plays a secondary part. One cannot say the same of all great painters." But in the opinion of Baudelaire, who was, perhaps unconsciously, the prophet of modern art, Ingres was only the victim of an obsession *"qui le contraint sans cesse à déplacer, à transposer et à altérer le beau"*.

The author of *Les Fleurs du Mal* saw in Ingres no longer the rival of David, but a more fortunate rival of young Delacroix. And here we should remember that when Baudelaire wrote that "the arts endeavour if not to fulfil themselves through one another, at least to lend one another new strength", he was certainly thinking of Delacroix.

With Delacroix we come to romanticism. This was not the camouflaged mediæval romanticism of Baron Leys, for whom, among the painters who interest us, only the ignoramus Van Gogh entertained an incomprehensible sympathy, nor the romanticism of more genuine painters such as Géricault, who imagined that, because they had renovated the subject-matter of their pictures, they had also reformed painting. Delacroix set out from the romantic principle that a picture "should above all reflect the artist's intimate thought, which must dominate the subject in the same way as a creator dominates his creation",[1] but he came to the conclusion, essentially a plastic one, that "light, shade reflections and atmosphere cannot be substituted by line and style". In this way he began the revolution in colour and this, incidentally, was helped on by the "discovery" of the Orient.

But the revolution of colour was above all due to the English: "Away, then, with greys, blacks, browns and all those bituminous colours used by the French landscape painters of the middle of the century, who seemed to look at nature through a black looking-glass!" cried Ruskin, the apostle of the Pre-Raphaelites and the first fervent admirer of the Primitives.

"Constable, that admirable man, one of England's glories", wrote

---

[1] Baudelaire, *L'Art Romantique*.

Delacroix in 1850; "I have spoken to you about him and the impression he made on me while I was painting the *Massacre of Chios*. He and Turner[1] are real reformers. Our school, which now abounds in men of talent similar to theirs, has greatly benefited by their example."

But Baron Gros thought that the *Massacre of Chios*,[2] which was inspired by one of his own most spectacular works, was a "massacre of painting".

At that time, as Baudelaire pointed out, Delacroix's name conjured up some vague idea of "misdirected ardour, turbulence, daring inspiration and even disorder". As Georges Duthuit has explained, Delacroix's genius had to content itself with being "smuggled through". But Delacroix's laws of colour,[3] based on the prism, were the first serious threat to "local tone" (the tone appropriate to the object painted)—one of the dogmas of what was misnamed "*l'Ecole*". An art critic, Paul Mantz, wrote of *La Barque du Christ*: "I did not realise that blue and green could be used in such a terrifying way."[4] It is amusing to think that even in the eyes of his contemporaries Delacroix's romanticism had nothing literary about it.

Before Delacroix had triumphed over Ingres, a new rival, Courbet, barred his way; and with Courbet realism forced the door of the *Ecole*. This was a new battle lost, since another of the dogmas on which the *Ecole* based its vain existence was that contemporary life did not deserve to inspire the artist. Theodore Rousseau, Diaz, Daubigny, Millet and Corot proved the contrary. Jean-Jacque's naturalism, which

---

[1] Later on, however, the conviction gained ground that Turner—during his "luminous" period— had been ahead of Monet in adopting the "colours of the prism". "You call them luminous", protested Renoir, "those colours like the ones used by pastrycooks to colour nougat and caramels? Come, come. It is just the same as when he used to paint with his chocolate. It is just the same thing" (Vollard, *Renoir*).

[2] "To paint the *Massacre of Chios* (1824), he had the courage to banish useless ochres and to use instead colours which were lively, intense and pure: cobalt blue, emerald green and madder lacquer" (Signac, *D'Eugène Delacroix au Néo-impressionisme*).

[3] We shall enumerate them later on. For the moment this appreciation by Eugène Veron must suffice: "Up to the last day of his life he studied the laws of complementary colours, their modifications due to light and the effects resulting from the contrast of tones. Delacroix often made use of the *mélange optique*, thereby giving the impression that he had used a colour which had never existed on his palette. He reached an extraordinary assurance in this field because over and above his natural talent he had knowledge and a mind. It is easy to observe that those of his works which are most admired for their colours are the ones in which the contrasts were obtained and made directly visible through daring brush-work" (quoted by Signac in *D'Eugène Delacroix au Néo-impressionisme*).

[4] Van Gogh, to his brother: "*La Barque du Christ:* I mean that painting in blues and greens with purple and red splashes and a little lemon yellow for the nimbus, the halo; the colours themselves speak a symbolic language."

had so delighted Marie-Antoinette, reanimated the souls of the painters and poets of the Second Empire. All of a sudden they were back at the tendencies which had been stifled by the Revolution of '89.

Parisians discovered that, besides the heroes of antiquity, Poussin's severe architecture and Claude Lorrain's majestic landscapes, also existed the no less poetic peasants and fields, valleys and woods and streams of Corot's pastoral nymphs. French artists rediscovered the people depicted by the Le Nains, or, rather, they rediscovered the poetry of the people, which in the eyes of some was purely agrarian, but for others had a rough strength only turned into violence by the operation of justice.

"A portrait by Courbet", wrote Van Gogh to his brother, "painted in all kinds of lovely deep russet tones, golden, with purple shadows all the colder because of the 'contrast' of black, and with a bit of white linen to rest the eye, has a value far superior, more energetic, freer and more beautiful than that of any portrait where the artist has tried to imitate the colour of the face with timid accuracy."

But Renoir was right when he said: "Courbet is still tradition. Manet is a new epoch in painting." It is impossible to think of Courbet as a revolutionary. When they admitted Courbet, the *Ecole* authorities resigned themselves to recognising an artist who reflected particular aspects and sentiments of the time, but they had no need to reproach him for his drawing and composition, and only a little for his use of colour.

This does not mean that the public had already accepted Courbet or Corot. The public did not even admire "Monsieur Ingres" as yet. And most people continued to look on Delacroix as "unruly and inaccurate, a criminal against colour". The fashionable painters of the time were Gérome and Baudry, men whose works, as Lionello Venturi wrote in his essay on *Impressionism*, were romances of the Georges Ohnet type—in other words, they had sunk to the level of "commercial statues in bronze and alabaster".

In his well-known book on the Impressionists, Théodore Duret shows how, at that time, there existed in the studios "a universally taught and practised technique for distributing light and shade on the canvas and for applying colours. It was inconceivable that light

7

could be introduced without necessarily and inevitably adding shade, or that bright colours could be used without intermediary half-tones." In this way painters ended by "painting only sombre pictures from which the splendour of vivid and brilliant colours had disappeared". It was these colours that Delacroix discovered afresh.

In 1863, at the *Salon des Refusés*—held by concession of Napoleon III's weak liberality—Manet provoked general horror with his *Déjeuner sur l'Herbe*. But at the same time he brought about one of the conditions for the rebirth of art—namely, the final break with the *Ecole*. He not only broke with the *Ecole*, but banished it for ever from the history of art. In vain the *Ecole* tried to resist, counting on the disgust Monet and Cézanne, Impressionism and Cubism, aroused in the public, the masses and the so-called élite. After the decisive turning point of 1863, the *Ecole* failed to produce a single French artist.

Something similar was happening in literature with Flaubert, Balzac and Zola. Stretching out a brotherly hand to Manet, Zola cried: "There are no more masters and no more schools. We are in the midst of anarchy and each one of us is a rebel who thinks, creates and fights for himself."

Then, with the defeat of Napoleon III, came political liberation and the age of democracy. Thanks to the French, for fifty years mankind was able to imagine it had reached a high level of civilisation. Admittedly, it only took the Germans a few weeks to carry us back to barbarism, but fortunately this is a matter which has nothing to do with our subject.

According to Théodore Duret and many others, the very substance of French national culture was transformed. The forms of art and literature were divorced from Latin classicism, or rather, as I should prefer to say, from academicism, from that "noisy emptiness" which long ago mortified the wise Petronius. For, after all, Cézanne was Latin in more than blood. And what about Renoir, and Picasso, and the Mediterranean Matisse?[1]

---

[1] Van Gogh to his brother: "I can well believe that a new school of colourists should spring up in the south as I realise more and more that the northern colourists rely too much on their ability with the brush and on picturesque effects rather than on a desire to express something through the medium of colour. Here, under a stronger sun, I see the truth of what Pissarro said to me—and Gauguin, too, wrote to me—about the simplicity, the colouring and the seriousness in these great effects of sunlight. In the north it would be impossible to imagine it."

8

But let us return to the year 1863 and to *Le Déjeuner sur l'Herbe*.[1] When he suppressed shade and painted *clair sur clair*, or merely used less vivid tones on the parts where others would have spread great dark patches, Manet returned, in a certain sense, to the origins of painting. For, with the use of chiaroscuro which brought the suggestion of a third dimension, from Giotto onwards painting had gradually encroached further and further into the domain of sculpture.

Two years later (at the Salon of 1865), the *Olympia* loosed an even greater flood of indignation. A gulf opened up that year between the artist and the public which has never since been bridged. The public was accustomed to seeing pictures as stories—whether heroic or merely agreeable. Man's innate interest in a work of art, as such, had been led astray and corrupted for centuries. As for colour, the public was more given to admiring the effect of layers of varnish than that of the actual colours—as though the pleasures of the mind had entirely given way to the pleasures of the palate which relished, in those shiny pastes, who knows what gluttonous memories! And it is still the same to-day, as one can see from the almost general disappointment experienced when a picture has been restored to its original colours.[2]

It is not difficult, therefore, to imagine how Paris received the *Olympia* in 1865. Because he attempted to defend Manet's work, Zola had to leave *L'Evènement*, a daily paper which later turned into the *Figaro*. In spite of the growth of some sincere understanding in the years that have passed since, the gulf between art and the people has

[1] "The significant picture in which Manet tries to conciliate the classical and the realistic idea," wrote Gino Severini in his book on figurative art, "is *Le Déjeuner sur l'herbe* (1863), a picture inspired by Giorgione's (or Titian's) *Concerto Campestre*. The composition was taken from an engraving by Raphael, but the figures were painted from life, one after the other. To-day, thanks to Mme. Ernest Rouart (*née* Manet), we know that Ferdinand Leenhoff, Gustave Manet and Victorine Meurand sat for this painting. Of all methods an artist can use this one is the most contrary to art. When he had composed the picture, Manet painted it from life, piece by piece, and this accounts for the infinite variety of treatment we detect as soon as we look at this picture. The figures are drawn with care and are thickly painted, whereas the inanimate objects are painted with rough strokes of the brush, hardly covering the canvas and in some places even leaving it bare. But for all that, Manet's miraculous talent gave this picture a certain unity, and it is particularly interesting to the critic since it reveals an enormous effort at renovation, an attempt to throw off the black shadows of the Spanish painters, and, following the example of the Venetians from whom this picture derived its inspiration, an endeavour to merge and identify tone and colour. Preoccupation with tone and colour was revealed for the first time, and for this reason it is of great importance to the critic."

[2] "In France people are rebellious against all innovations in art and they are not only insensitive, but hostile to colour" (Signac).

"I fully realise that to be a colourist can be more damaging than helpful. . . . One needs more active senses, and a deeper sensitiveness so as to recognise mistakes, discords and false relations between colours and lines" (Delacroix).

always remained. This is a sad admission to make, and I hasten to add that the gulf has not been fatal to art. Far from it!

In the year Manet exhibited *Le Déjeuner sur l'herbe*, Monet, Renoir, Sisley and Bazille were meeting in Gleyre's studio. Pissarro met Monet in 1857, and made the acquaintance of Cézanne a little later. "In 1865, Monet, Bazille, Renoir, Sisley, Pissarro and Cézanne met Manet, as well as Baudelaire and Gambetta, at the Lejones' house. In 1866 Cézanne introduced Zola to Manet at the Café Guerbois; Manet had other *avant-garde* around him, including painters—Degas, and a few critics, such as Huysmans, Duranty and Duret. In 1865 Pissarro was thirty-five, Manet thirty-three, Sisley twenty-eight, Cézanne twenty-six, Monet twenty-five and Renoir and Bazille were both twenty-four. Sisley and Cézanne contributed their literary culture to the group. They all studied Fontainebleau and its interpreters, Corot and Rousseau. They all admired Courbet, and Renoir had a weakness for Diaz. At the 1866 Salon, Manet, Sisley, Bazille and Berthe Morisot exhibited, but Cézanne was refused. Manet reaped scandal, Courbet success."[1]

The following year Manet held a one-man show outside the precincts of the universal exhibition. "He treats figure-painting in a way which the schools only allow in still-life work", said Zola when he analysed this most refined of realists. But Zola, as Lionello Venturi justly remarked, failed to understand that "in a still-life there could be as many moral and 'poetic' values as in a religious painting, and he did not foresee that his friend Cézanne would later be able to create a tremendous drama with a few onions on a table".[2]

Meanwhile, Claude Monet had already discovered the road to Impressionism. From as early as 1830 there had been a fashion among landscape painters of studying Nature from life and then composing the picture in the studio. This was what Cézanne later called: *"plein' air d'appartement"*. "In 1865 Monet painted a picture out of doors in the garden. He repeated this experiment again in 1867. At first this pretence irritated Courbet and Manet, but a few years later Manet followed his example."[3]

[1] L. Venturi, *op. cit.*   [2] L. Venturi, *ibid.*
[3] Courbet exhibited *Le Combat des Cerfs* in 1861. Telemaco Signorini, Cristiano Banti, and Vicenzo Cabianco arrived in Paris, where Nino Costa already lived. The next year the Italians returned to Florence and in the name of nature and truth started a revolt against the authority of the academies.

1874 saw the first exhibition of Impressionist painters at the gallery of the photographer Nadar in the Boulevard des Capucines—of course, the term "Impressionist" had not yet come into existence. The painters who, in 1863, had obtained a room for "rejected pictures" on the premises of the Salon itself formed the nucleus of the group. Whistler, Bracquemond, Jongkind, Fantin-Latour and Renoir were joined by many others, among them Degas and the Italian, Giuseppe de Nittis. And these last were led by the Monet-Manet bloc which had become stronger from the day Monet had succeeded in persuading the "hispan-ising" Manet to discover the joys of painting out of doors. Cézanne contributed *La Maison du Pendu*, which was later bought by Count de Camondo and now hangs in the Louvre. The title of one of Manet's pictures gave birth to the disparaging epithet "Impressionist", a term subsequently adopted, in the heat of discussion, by the defenders of the movement themselves. It was during these years that black, which Tintoretto called the queen of colours, was discarded by Monet because "it did not exist in nature". Later on Van Gogh, though not an Impressionist, even went as far as saying that black did not necessarily exist as a colour.

The second exhibition was in 1876. The third, at which the exhibitors called themselves "Impressionists", was on April 23, 1877. This was the last exhibition at which the Impressionists appeared as a complete group. It took place at 6 rue le Peletier. Two hundred and forty-six pictures were hung on the walls of a house under repair. "They have to be seen to be believed", wrote the *Chronique des Arts et des Curiosités*; "they make one laugh and weep at the same time. They reveal utter ignorance of draughtsmanship, composition and colour. Children obtain better results when they play with paper and paints." But Paul Mantz defined, if not Impressionism itself, at least "the Impressionist painter" as "sincere and free". The Impressionist, he realised, "submits in the ingenuousness of his heart to the absolute

---

Cescioni, Borrani, Lega, Morandi and Abbati formed a group known as the "rustics". The discussions in the Café Michelangelo, the rustics' Florentine headquarters, did not equal those of the Café Guerbois, where Manet reigned with Monet and Cézanne on either side. And even if news of the Paris group reached the Italians, who had the opportunity of seeing two Delacroix in a Florentine collection, the Italian revolution was independent of the French one, and did not bear the same fruits. One should not underestimate Fattori's natural talent, Signorini's intelligence and Lega's forcefulness. But in a provincial country such as Italy was at that time they could not hope to attain a truly plastic language.

fascination emanating from nature", and translates, "in all simplicity and frankness, the intensity of the impression received". Rivière was full of indignation at the ignoramuses who made fun of Cézanne's *Baigneuses*: he said they were like barbarians criticising the Parthenon.

Now, what was meant by "translating in all simplicity and frankness, the intensity of the impression received"? "The impressionist's innovation", wrote Duranty in 1876, "really consists in their discovery that light discolours tones, that the sun reflected from objects tends, by virtue of clarity, to bring them back to the luminous unity which fuses its seven prismatic rays into one colourless state—namely, light. Proceeding intuitively, the Impressionists gradually managed to break up solar light into its component elements, its rays, and then to recompose its unity by means of the general harmony of iridescences which these rays distribute on the canvas." In other words, the Impressionists carried Delacroix's laws of colour to their logical conclusion. At Saint-Denis du Saint-Sacrement, Delacroix, who wanted to paint a picture worthy of the great Venetian colourists, had been obliged to do the white lights in pure chrome yellow and the half-tints in Prussian blue: "Opaque orange in the light colours, the most brilliant purples in the shadows, and golden reflections in the shadows reflected from the ground." Thus the Impressionists not only succeeded in freeing themselves from slavery to subject-matter and photographic likeness, which they replaced by "character", following Manet's example; they also rediscovered an ancient technique (though they understandably thought it was their own invention) which consisted in no longer mixing colours on the palette, and then on the canvas, but in letting the colours be mixed by the eye, according to the recently discovered laws of *le mélange optique*.[1] In other words, the real picture was not the picture painted by the artist, but the one which impressed itself on the retina of the spectator's eye. This was to be the real innovation of Neo-Impressionism and Divisionism.

[1] A *mélange optique* is a fusion of colour-lights. For example, the fusion of luminous rays of different colours at the same point of a surface. Obviously, the painter does not paint with rays of light. However, just as the physical scientist can recompose the phenomenon of optical fusion by means of a disc, divided into segments of different colours, which rotates rapidly, so the painter can obtain this fusion by means of the juxtaposition of little multicoloured dabs. On the rotating disc, or on the painter's canvas seen from a certain distance, the eye does not distinguish the coloured segments or the brush-dabs, but the sum total of their lights—that is to say, the optical fusion of the colours of the segments or the optical fusion of the colours of the brush-dabs (Signac, *op. cit.*).

12

Later, after he had attained success, Monet said that the Impressionists painted "as a bird sings". This is true, to some degree, of Renoir, Pissarro, Sisley and one or two others. But it is not true of Monet, although he was the soul of the group. Monet seems to me to have been a kind of Icarus of the Impressionist world. For him Nature was not, as for Delacroix, a "dictionary" in which the artist can at most look up the correct words and leave the rest to his imagination— "which has taught man the moral values of colour". Nor did he attempt to humanise Nature like Millet. (If, as Van Gogh maintained, Millet's peasants look as though they have been painted with the earth they are sowing, then it necessarily follows that the earth is the very flesh of the peasants.) Nor did Monet, like Courbet, think that the realist painter who wishes to live among the people and their miseries, in the snowy forests and golden dawns of his time, should only be inspired by the visible world. And, unlike Manet, Monet did not want to force Nature to become classical. After 1880 Cézanne managed to resolve the dual problem of light and colour by making a synthesis of both. But in 1875 and the following years Monet was obsessed with exactly the problem which tormented Gauguin many years later in his distant exile: "Shall I live long enough to gather all this light, all this joy of sunlight?"[1] Except that Gauguin, like Renoir, but in his own way, was above all thinking of the golden forms he saw in all that light. Then was there no one to warn Monet of his error? There must have been someone. There is always an informed chorus round the blind hero of a great tragedy. But in life, as in drama, the warnings of the chorus are of no avail.

The main reason for the public's dislike of the Impressionists (except in the case of Cézanne, who met with particularly violent antagonism) was their choice of subjects, as Venturi has pointed out. Art lovers came from the aristocracy and the middle classes, and in the years following the Commune they were in full reaction. "Moreover, it did not escape their notice that a new social content had consciously or unconsciously crept into the Impressionists' painting. Renoir's charm belonged, not to the boulevards, but to the suburbs; Pissarro's peasants were 'vulgar', and you could see their resemblance to the characters

[1] Degas said: "Painting was first of all coffee, then white coffee, then milk."

13

in *Les Misérables*; Monet's revolutionary energy steamed out of his locomotives, and Cézanne's spirit was obviously anarchical and related to Zola's. In other words, Impressionism brought to painting something of what, in the political life of France, was called *la fin des notables*, the end of refinement and splendour, the beginning of a new dignity for the humble classes." The hostility diminished, as Venturi might have observed, with the increasing spread of confidence in the Third Republic.

And now Cézanne no longer took part in exhibitions of Impressionists. Certainly their friendship had been useful to him, for they had encouraged him to study Nature and to paint in the open, but he could not hold with their theories on breaking up light, which gradually became as dogmatic and dangerous as the famous "local tone" canons of the *Ecole*. Cézanne, in his own words, tried to *refaire Poussin sur nature*—that is, he tried to discover, through correct tone-values, the sense of form which had been utterly betrayed by the *Ecole*. Seurat tried in vain to save Impressionism, but Cézanne's instinct triumphed over the great "Divisionist's" scientific knowledge.

Many artists saw in Impressionism merely an advance on preceding tendencies in art, an advance crystallised in the line and colour compromise. Degas (1834–1917) was brutally torn from the academic traditionalism of the *coulisses* and the unscented ballet-dancers. Even without the help of Impressionism and its liberation of colours from the tyranny of shadow, his pastels would probably have been just as admirable. Degas was a genuine artist who would have brought exceptional sensitiveness even to academic painting. But Impressionism renovated his palette, taught him to choose his own subjects freely and enabled him to express his true nature. From the academies he had learnt to discover the gracefulness of the human body, but Impressionism revealed to him its power and its sensual drama. Henri de Toulouse-Lautrec was another great artist who was indebted to the Impressionists for his palette. He died in 1901 when he was only thirty-seven years old. He had a strong influence on the early Picasso. Lautrec was an illustrator and caricaturist of great genius, but like Daumier, he is more admired for his ability as a satirist than as a painter. His message, in which we can often detect a note of Goya, could have been transmitted even without the medium of pure colours.

Tradition and Nature

THE problem Cézanne (1839–1906) set himself can be summed up in one of the controversial maxims attributed to him by his friends and disciples: *refaire Poussin sur nature*. In an article published in 1920, Severini justly expressed his amazement that intelligent painters and men of culture should have discussed the literal sense of this maxim without realizing its meaninglessness. A more recent critic, Lionello Venturi, maintains that Cézanne must have said: "*vivifier Poussin sur nature*", and to support this he quotes a letter dated September 13, 1903, to a young painter, Camoin, in which Cézanne said: "Couture (Manet's master) used to say to his pupils: 'Keep good company—in other words go to the Louvre. But when you have looked at the great masters who dwell there quietly, you must hurry out and stimulate the instincts and art perceptions which lie within you through contact with nature'". Consequently what Cézanne meant was not "to recreate or reanimate" Poussin, but that art should bring to life, by studying nature, "*les instincts, les sensations d'art*" innate in the artist. (A young philosopher, Bergson, who was soon to rise to world fame and who in those days was writing about art for the newspapers, defined the artist as "a man whose soul vibrates in unison with nature"). Cézanne, like his friend Pissarro, thought a museum was a necropolis, a cemetery from which the artist should hurry away. Not that he despised the lessons taught by the great masters. On the contrary, no one studied and copied their works in the Louvre more assiduously than he did. But he knew how much art had come to suffer from the excessive subservience to tradition enforced by *l'Ecole*. Moreover we must never forget that Cézanne was an Impressionist, even though for him (and for Renoir) Impressionism was a means and not the end it was for Manet and Pissarro. But none of this explains how that saying, *refaire Poussin sur nature*, to which we attach so much importance, ever arose. It cannot have been "*vivifier*" because there is only one way to vivify Poussin—by removing the layers of varnish which have been accumulated by the prudence of curators.

Obviously the maxim must not be taken literally. It is ridiculous to think of "recreating" or "reanimating" Poussin or Veronese, and Cézanne was not a fool. But it is such a typical Cézanne saying, so precise and synthetic in its terms. To many of us it seems to convey to perfection the meaning of Cézanne's work, and if it were not already in existence, we might have invented it ourselves.

As I was saying, only a fool could think of being able to "recreate" Poussin or Veronese even *sur nature*. Why did Cézanne, who was above all sensitive to the movement and colour of the Venetians, say Poussin in particular? It may be, as Venturi suggests, that the saying implies a criticism of that great Frenchman's work. But I am inclined to think that the whole business is far more simple and at the same time far more profound.

Poussin was the last and the most famous of the great French "classical painters". *Refaire Poussin sur nature* therefore can reasonably only mean one thing: Let us discover a new classical art based on nature. Poussin was responsible for pointing out the way. In a letter, a sort of spiritual testament, written to Monsieur de Noyer (Venturi also quotes this letter, though in an essay on Renoir) Poussin said: "There are two ways of looking at objects: one is simply to look at them, the other is to look at them attentively. Simply to look at them is no more than to receive naturally upon the eye the shape and appearance of the object in question. But to look at an object attentively means, over and above the simple and natural impression made upon the eye, to find out carefully the way of knowing the object well. Thus it can be said that to *look* at a thing is a natural function, whereas what I should call '*seeing*' it is a rational process."

From his youth, Cézanne had aspired to the greatness of the classical masters; not, like his friend Zola, to fame alone. He believed in the need for theory. "In art," he said, "all is theory, applied and developed according to the teaching of nature"; and in his work he demonstrated the soundness of Poussin's assertions.

There is another saying of Cézanne's which is a corollary to the one quoted above: "to make Impressionism a museum art"—that is to say, an art worthy of museums. As I wrote in 1936 in my book on Cézanne, these two *boutades* which some people find contradictory and even meaningless, express the total of Cézanne's æsthetics—avoidance of the lifelessness of the Neo-Classicists and of the improvisation of the Impressionists, in other words, avoidance of the dead rules of the *Ecole* and the triviality of the Impressionists.

The letter to Camoin is certainly useful, but I think it expresses Couture's mentality more than Cézanne's, and it could equally well have been written by Manet, while the saying: *refaire Poussin sur nature*, could only have come from Cézanne.

Even the earliest compositions he painted when he was a pupil at the Swiss Academy—which are generally considered grotesque—make it evident that in all his work Cézanne aspired to the greatness of the past. From Loubon, his first teacher, Cézanne had learnt to paint *à la Courbet*, so to say, with "violent contrasts of light and shade",[1] but his heart leaned towards Delacroix. Delacroix was less unmindful than others of his age of the Italian and Spanish tradition—that is, of the greatness of the past. Cézanne became enthusiastic over Delacroix's romanticism, which, as we have seen, had nothing in common with the romanticism of Lamartine, Vigny, Hugo and of satellite painters, even if it was not the "supernaturalism" Delacroix described it as being in his famous letter to Heinrich Heine. However, while Monet was content with painting sea- and landscapes and trying to learn the secret of values from one or the other of his two masters, Boudin (the delicate landscape painter—tormented because he could not reproduce the splendour of the sky) and Jongkind the Dutch Pre-Impressionist (the first painter to break up colours and to split up his brush-strokes to an infinite degree, so as to obtain unusual colour effects "by juxtaposing multiple and almost pure pigments"),[2] Cézanne was busy emulating the great masters—above all, El Greco and Veronese. Venturi, going against Cézanne's own opinion and that of his contemporaries, says that from then onwards, like many great painters including Titian and Velasquez, Cézanne "was a great technician before being a true artist".

[1] L. Venturi, *op. cit.*
[2] All these merits were attributed to Jongkind by Signac, the theorist of "Divisionism".

17

Finally, Manet's star rose on Cézanne's uncertain horizon.

Like Cézanne, Manet had felt the fascination of museums more than the appeal of Nature. He never possessed what Cézanne called *le tempérament* (or creative force), but he had an unmistakable personality, easily recognisable even in works inspired by the Spanish painters. The Spanish influence helped to make what is known as his "black period", for at that time black, the "queen of colours", dominated his palette. When Cézanne and his Impressionist friends first met Manet he had already become a kind of hero through the scandal of *Le Déjeuner sur l'herbe*. Manet's Parisian character was profoundly irritating to the Provençal Cézanne, who was inclined by nature to be somewhat austere and taciturn. But how was Cézanne to withstand Manet's moral authority? "If", as Renoir confessed, "in spite of copying Velasquez and Goya, Manet was the forerunner and standard-bearer of our group, this was because he applied better than anyone else the simple formula we were all striving after." But this formula, though simple, was also serious. It meant the search for "character" which afterwards became, as we have already seen, the second of the two principles held by the Impressionists, who were opposed to photographic likeness in painting.

Manet abandoned the use of chiaroscuro and discovered a strong liking for painting pictures without much shading, almost in the flat. By using direct and violent lighting he obtained, though somewhat arbitrarily, a neat "contour" round the object, and freed it from the fastidious ambiguity of the chiaroscuro painters. "The tone spits!" said Cézanne admiringly when speaking of Manet, but what impressed him more than the tone was the "contour" and the consequent interplay of lines producing depth. From Manet Cézanne contracted the obsession with contour which lasted all his life and never gave him any peace.

But Manet's immediate influence on Cézanne's work was negligible. It marked the transition from his romantic to his Impressionist period. This once reached, Cézanne became indifferent to Manet's subsequent development. But when Manet had become with Monet joint leader of the Impressionist group, he added a remarkable series to his list of masterpieces already comprising *Le Balcon, Le Déjeuner à l'Atelier*

(1869) and the portrait of his pupil, the virginal Berthe Morisot, "the last elegant and 'feminine' painter we have had in France since Fragonard".[1] Manet now went on to paint *Sur la Plage* (1873), *Le Linge* (1875), *Chez le Père Lathuille* (1879) and finally the famous *Bar aux Folies Bergères*, which dates from about the end of 1881, a year and a half before his death.

Pissarro, whose friendship had been so profitable to the youthful Monet, exercised a strong influence on Cézanne in 1873, at Auvers. Pissarro was born in the Antilles, of a Creole mother and a French Jewish father. Cézanne underwent Pissarro's influence "so profoundly", writes Lionello Venturi, "that he finally freed himself from romanticism and in some way discovered his real self". There is a letter from Cézanne to his mother dating from this period. In it there is a touch of vanity, a very rare defect in Cézanne, proving that he had now reached maturity. "Pissarro", he writes, "thinks well of me. I am beginning to feel that I am better than the others around me, and you know that I have only reached this good opinion of myself conscientiously. I must go on working hard, but not to achieve that kind of limited stuff imbeciles so admire. . . ."

Cézanne found his true character by adopting the Impressionist technique, though for him it was only a starting point. Good painters, like Monet or Renoir, firmly believed in his genius. Henceforward— after the scandal caused by his participation in the 1877 exhibition —he was able to renounce the world and to withdraw from the Paris intellectuals who took pleasure in deprecating him. He now shut himself up and devoted himself to his own work. Emile Zola, his childhood friend, inflicted a final, undoubtedly bitter, blow upon him. As a young man, Zola had been in Cézanne's confidence, and knew the overwhelming exuberance of the Lycée schoolboy who sensed the beauty of the pine tree, which "*sur le bord de l'Arc planté, avançait sa tête chevelue sur le gouffre qui s'étendait à ses pieds*". In the past Zola had even reproached him for writing mostly about poetry in his letters, not enough about painting and sculpture. But now, genuinely distressed at not finding his friend among officially recognised painters, Zola took Cézanne as model for the character of an unsuccessful artist

[1] Renoir (to Vollard).

19

in his novel *L'Œuvre*, that of a man born with talent, who failed because of his inability to become a good craftsman. As a man, Cézanne had his faults. The need to live on a tiny income made him extremely avaricious, and if ever during the last years of his life he happened to give a penny to a beggar, he never failed to tell his son about it. But this fault notwithstanding, his soul was noble and proud, and when he received his copy of Zola's book, he merely thanked the famous author and begged to shake hands with him *"en songeant aux anciennes années"* and *"sous l'impulsion des temps écoulés"*. Obviously he must have suffered bitterly—above all, now he was aware of his own worth—at finding himself betrayed by his childhood friend, by the man who had been Manet's staunch defender and who always championed the misunderstood and the oppressed. Yet Cézanne would have been the first to forgive. It was Zola who was responsible for the final break, for he went so far as to avoid Cézanne when, many years later, a triumphal tour brought him to Aix.

Cézanne has been reproached for withdrawing into himself, but I incline to share Thierry Maulnier's opinion that "a man can only attain his deepest vital intensity, his universality and his essence by renouncing the world, withdrawing into himself, and devoting himself to himself, to his passions and his reason". Even if this is not true always, it certainly was for Cézanne during the years between 1878 and 1894. In the latter year the Caillebotte scandal again kindled controversy round his name. But by this time he had succeeded *"à faire de l'impressionisme une chose durable"* and *"à refaire Poussin sur nature"*. He had discovered his formal technique which will live as long as mankind continues to feel the need for art; and he had created a magnificent body of work.

It is impossible to describe the peculiarities of Cézanne's achievement briefly, so we must be content with a few short notes. In Cézanne's work, drawing and painting are no longer two separate elements of the picture, but a single element. "One draws as one paints", wrote Cézanne, "and this cannot be achieved without a good method of construction." As he said later:[1] "If a strong perception of nature—and mine is indeed acute—is the necessary basis for every conception

[1] In a letter to Louis Aurenche dated January 25, 1904.

of art, and one on which the future greatness and beauty of the work depends, a knowledge of the methods by which to express our emotions is no less necessary, and this is only acquired through long experience." "One must penetrate what one sees and strive to express oneself as logically as possible", he said to Emile Bernard, because "only nature, and the eye which educates itself by contact with nature, can bring about this progress". And it was also to Emile Bernard that he wrote the letter which later became the justification of Cubism: "*Traitez la nature par le cylindre, la sphère, le cône, le tout mis en perspective, soit que chaque côté d'un plan se dirige vers un point central. Les lignes parallèles à l'horizon donnent l'étendue, soit une section de la nature, ou, si vous aimez mieux, du spectacle que Pater Omnipotens Aeterne Deus étale devant nos yeux. Les lignes perpendiculaires à cet horizon donnent la profondeur. Or, la nature, pour nous hommes, est plus en profondeur qu'en surface, d'où la nécessité d'intro-duire dans nos vibrations de lumière, representés par le rouge et le jaune, une somme suffisante de bleutés, pour faire sentir l'air.*"

The outcome of his love and study of nature, Cézanne's work—in which "never was line so imbued with life, never was a stroke of the brush more based upon an ideal construction"[1] although it was planned in the flat (in other words, without the use of chiaroscuro)— reveals a systematic understanding of plastic form. And this plastic form reaches "a depth perhaps only attained by Rembrandt", to use the words of Roger Fry, one of Cézanne's authoritative commentators. I do not agree with Fry on all points. He also says that "the forms are in some way suggested to the spectator's imagination and demand his collaboration". But if this were true, Cézanne would not be a very great artist who, in his portraits, his harlequins and his card-players, is truly classical with a new and genuine classicism. The only col-laboration a picture by Cézanne requires from the spectator is that he should discard all his preconceived prejudices. He will then see the picture in its plastic truth, that of a geometry which may be somewhat elementary, but is nevertheless extraordinarily living and adequate.

In Cézanne's work, Delacroix's problem of colour and Monet's problem of light find their logical solution. "An optical sensation",

[1] Venturi, *Cézanne.*

wrote Cézanne,[1] "which is produced in our organ of sight makes us classify the planes represented by colour sensations into light, half-tones and quarter-tones (light therefore does not exist for the painter)." When he did away with the problem of chiaroscuro and related it to the problem of colour ("Light and shade are colour relations: these two principal attributes differ, not in their general intensity, but in their individual sonority"), Cézanne was obliged—with rudimentary knowledge but sure instinct—to face the problem of space. This led him to the discovery (miraculous in an artist who only had a vague notion of perspective and music) of volume and rhythm.[2] "Cézanne", says Severini, "made use of the contrast of masses, and of simultaneous contrast: each mass is divided into a greater or lesser number of pictorial values which blend in the general orchestration, though each vibrates separately. Thus there is no square inch in his paintings which does not glitter like a precious stone." This description sets me thinking of mosaic work.

Such were the main points of the grammar Cézanne imparted, towards the end of his life, to a few young painters like Bernard and Camoin, who seemed to him to be particularly suited to understand it. But it was only after his death and with the Fauves and the Cubists that it reached its inevitable synthesis.

Towards the end of 1895 when Vollard's initiative enabled people to see a large collection of Cézanne's paintings, the now comfortably established Impressionists had already forgotten all the suffering they had endured through their first fifteen years, years in which they battled tooth and nail against public hostility. The pig-headed loyalty of the earliest collectors had overcome the diffidence of the critics. (The same thing has been happening almost invariably ever since: hence the decline of criticism.) Impressionism (which the Divisionists were speedily revising, as we shall see) had become the new grammar of painting in Europe. Theo van Rysselberghe came to Paris from Belgium, Max Libermann from Germany. They were only two of the many painters from abroad who now congregated in the French capital.

---

[1] To Bernard, March 23, 1904.
[2] His famous distortions of photographic likeness were required by the plastic logic of pictures which started out from imitation to reach in the end a new plastic reality. But Cézanne never went beyond human boundaries.

Within the space of one generation the anarchy of the preceding period was succeeded, perhaps too prematurely, by a new order.

Renoir (1841–1919) was one of the first to rebel against Impressionist conformism. *La Loge* (1874), *La Baigneuse*, now at the Moscow Museum, *Le Déjeuner des Canotiers* (1881), and above all *Le Moulin de la Galette*, at the Louvre, were real masterpieces for Impressionism. And when he painted the portraits of Mme Charpentier and Mlle Savary, who were in some degree arbiters of intellectual and social life at the time, Renoir contributed enormously to the success of his Impressionist friends. But during a brief visit to Italy he discovered Carpaccio (" a great painter", he said to Vollard, "whose colours are fresh and living, and who was one of the first who dared to paint the ordinary man and woman in the street"), Raphael and the mosaics in St. Mark's. In short, he felt the "call of the classics". In his case, the call was somewhat vain, but it enabled him to break with the Impressionists and to return to studio painting, though he never went back to the "black" painting, *à la Courbet*, of his youth.

It was not that Renoir reproached Impressionism for not providing real spiritual emotion, or, rather, for not combining the pleasures of the eye with those of the mind. Renoir loathed "spirituality" in art, the kind of spirituality we find in El Greco, for example, which recurs again in Cézanne. But Renoir loved nature too much to be able to study it with the cold determination of his friend Cézanne. He surrendered to the joy of attempting to rival, with his tubes of paint, the colours on the palette of the sky. Even in the ancient masters he disliked figures which appeared to be thinking about something. What he loved was the vacant look in the eyes of Raphael madonnas, and Ingres's allegorical *Source*. Anything pertaining to the flesh, anything lovely to look on and to touch exalted his imagination and gave him a joy no less pure and intense than the kind of joy Euclid must have experienced when solving his absurd problems. Renoir's painting, unlike Cézanne's, appears sensual to some critics. His *baigneuses*, they maintain, are "*tout à fait tournées du côté du plaisir*". But in a work of art, even sensuality arouses pure emotion in the spectator. True enough, Iago, in *Othello*, when speaking of beauty and intelligence, says:

23

"The one's for use, the other uses it."

But Iago was only an impostor and a timid dilettante of deception.

So as to obtain a natural effect Renoir, like all the Impressionists, used blues, violets and purples for shading; the golden transparency of trees was there *"à faire mes tableaux"*, as he said to Vollard. Once he was back in his studio, with normal lighting, things were no longer the same. The golden transparency of his trees had not prevented him from painting masterpieces. But the truth of the matter was that Renoir's passion for what was "epidermic" had brought him to love the texture of painting and even the material of his picture. Moreover, he was right in saying that in the *Marriage of Cana*, in Titian's nudes and in Rembrandt's portraits we find a very different kind of light, *"autrement chouetté"*, from the light in Impressionist painting. "When we look at a picture by Rembrandt do we feel the need to ask whether it was painted indoors or out of doors?"

Renoir returned to tradition, and ended by denying the possibility of progress in painting; and in this he was not altogether wrong, since thought in general and art particularly cannot be subordinated in a hierarchy based exclusively on method. No one admired Cézanne more than Renoir did, but nature had showered talents upon him, and even the hardships he had to face in life (as a boy he had been obliged to earn his living by decorating porcelain and fans) had taught him special knowledge of his craft. As for theories—he was only interested in rather primitive ones expounded by Cennini which he came across by chance. Painting, for Renoir, was like breathing. His remarkable work was achieved by renouncing systems and programmes, and by concentrating endlessly on perfecting the colours as a pioneer—they were later adopted by almost all the other painters of the time, including Degas. Though inferior to Cézanne in one way, Renoir's work, considered in itself, surpasses Cézanne in another—in its extraordinary felicity. A mere film of colour enveloping the object was enough to indicate its basic proportions. Like Cézanne, Renoir achieved his architectural effect without the use of chiaroscuro. But while Cézanne turned the younger generation in a fresh direction, Renoir was content to be a great master, and only asked to be admired.

He has been called a woman's painter, but saying that means just nothing.

Renoir did not believe in a new kind of art, whereas Cézanne, who admired Baudelaire, did. To a young poet, Gasquet, Cézanne even wrote: "Perhaps I have come too soon. I was the painter of your generation rather than of my own."

"When will men understand the meaning of the word *freedom*?" wondered Gauguin. Renoir understood it. As Lionello Venturi has pointed out, once he had freed himself from systems, he began to want to free himself from nature. Renoir discovered "a new freedom of style, attained without a programme, but in accordance with his own nature, like the blossoming of a flower or the ripening of a fruit".

Two Rival Æsthetics

ALTHOUGH the date 1895, with which I began this survey, is so significant in the life of Cézanne, the Master of Aix, and in the evolution of modern art, we must not imagine that Cézanne's first one-man show, arranged by Vollard, made an immediate challenge to the widespread convictions of the Impressionist movement. For from 1870 onwards Impressionism continuously exercised "a salubrious and brilliant influence"[1] on all painters, with the exception of Eugène Carrière, Fantin-Latour and Gustave Moreau,[2] who formed a trio of "*isolés*". As we look back over the last fifty years, 1895 is an essential landmark. For all that, the critics, collectors and artists who first admired Cézanne were not to know that this date marked the beginning of one of the most "troubled" periods in European art. On the contrary, to them it represented a stupendous "conclusion" reached by the proudest and most independent of the Impressionists.

In 1895 two rival tendencies competed for the attention of the young generation: Neo-Impressionism or Divisionism, and the Symbolism of the *Nabis* or Pont-Aven school. Later, Divisionism and Symbolism, as well as Fauvism, focused interest on Cézanne. It was only after they had lost all faith in the future of Seurat's and Gauguin's æsthetics that young painters, the masters of contemporary painting, Matisse, Picasso and Braque, turned to the work of the great recluse. We must also remember that Matisse's first important participation in a general exhibition dates from only a few months after Cézanne's personal show.

Nevertheless, even during the first years of this century it was not

[1] C. Mauclair, *L'Impressionisme*.
[2] "Certainly there are vivid colours in it, but they can hardly be seen through the veil spread by modesty. Lovingly, little girls beg for tenderness with their outstretched and caressing hands: it must be a picture by Carrière" (Gauguin, *Avant et Après*).
The collective portraits by Fantin-Latour are not without historical and documentary value.
Gustave Moreau, whom the Impressionists loathed, held official appointments, but no one was interested in knowing how or what he painted. He later became Rouault's and Matisse's teacher.

Cézanne, but Impressionism, which attracted Severini, Modigliani and Picasso to Paris. In 1909 the Futurists still believed Divisionism was the last word. So Boccioni set about "solidifying" Impressionism in all seriousness: perhaps he had not yet heard of Seurat and Cézanne, who had set out to do the same thing thirty years earlier. This should not surprise us unduly, because, in spite of the rather spectacular part the Impressionists played in the great Paris Exhibition of 1900, it was not until the World War of 1914 that the public really began to admire their work, and by this time Arp and the poet, Tristan Tzara, were busy launching Dada. The same thing happened with Cubism. By the time the so-called élite had begun to discuss it and accept it, the artists responsible for the movement had already gone back, in perplexity, to an "imitative" kind of painting. Recently we have had a return to Cubism, and doubtless this new Cubism will only be understood, I will not venture to say "discussed", in twenty years' time. By then, no doubt, Kandinsky's "concrete" work, the second period of abstract painting, will have become generally accepted.

Seurat and Signac exhibited for the first time in 1886, at the last exhibition the Impressionists gave as a group.[1] Their pictures were "painted solely in pure pigments distinguished and harmonised by optical fusion, following a thought-out technique".

Georges Seurat (1859–91) sent in to this exhibition a picture which I consider to be his first and greatest masterpiece, *Un Dimanche à la Grande Jatte*. It is painted with the Divisionist technique which he was the first to introduce. Camille Pissarro, who worked in all kinds of styles (and thus was a forerunner of Picasso), Lucien Pissarro his son, and Paul Signac, the apostle of Divisionism, contributed paintings technically somewhat similar.

Un Dimanche à la Grande Jatte, done at the age of twenty-five (Seurat

[1] The Venetian painter, Zandomeneghi, who had taken part in all the Impressionists' exhibitions since 1879, also exhibited at this one. If Zandomeneghi, who was obviously a more genuine painter than De Nittis or Boldini, had been able to rid himself of an element of bad taste and Italian provincialism, he would not have been easily eclipsed by the fame of Renoir and Degas. As for De Nittis (who was not an Impressionist perhaps because, in his anxiety for success, he was unwilling to defy public opinion which was still unfavourable to Impressionism), it is worth mentioning that he was the first painter of the Nadar group to rush to London, and there his portraits and landscapes reached fabulous prices. And when, many years later, Degas was exhibited in London, critics heralded this great French painter as a good pupil of De Nittis. Boldini's Parisian period seems to me to afford a brilliant example of everything that should be strictly avoided in painting. The "rustics", from whom De Pisis derived, were better painters.

died when he was only thirty-two), has had a wide influence on modern art. Even to-day Campigli's wistful human frameworks remind one of the figures in *La Grande Jatte*, enclosed in their hieratic pattern, living and concise human structures evolved from the science of angles and straight and curved lines which Seurat seems to have inherited from the Chinese rather than from Delacroix. Indeed, certain of his compositions, so scientifically perfect, do make one think of Chinese painting.[1]

"Here", wrote Van Gogh from Arles to his brother, "Seurat would find extremely picturesque human figures in spite of their modern clothes." And indeed, Seurat's "elegant living structures" were inspired by the fashion, *si simplement arrondie*, of 1884. In other words, they were not arbitrary, like Campigli's; at most they could be described as "lyrically geometrised" like Paolo Uccello's battle scenes.

It was as if Seurat, who hardly knew the Impressionists, had been entrusted by Delacroix with the secret of the laws of colour, which a scientist, Chevreul, later classified in his *Laws of Simultaneous Contrast.*[2]

Delacroix had not foreseen all their possibilities. He boasted that he could paint the most resplendent female nude with mud—maintaining that colour in itself signified nothing since it was the adjacent colours which caused, by contrast, its luminosity or opacity—and was reluctant to abandon his muddy colours. The result is that, as Signac pointed out, *L'Entrée des Croisés* would now appear sombre if placed between Renoir's *Déjeuner des Canotiers* and Seurat's *Le Cirque*, which are done in pure colour.

Whereas Delacroix had desperately tried to *faire de la lumière avec des couleurs boueuses*,[3] the Impressionists simplified their palette and made it simple and pure.

Thus the Impressionist painters relinquished smooth painting which then required mixed colours and inaugurated prismatic colour painting, breaking up their brush strokes into minute dabs or commas, *pailles dansantes* as Jules Laforgue called them—their counterpart to Delacroix's vibrant brush strokes or *hachures*.

---

[1] As Georges Duthuit rightly observed in his *Peinture moderne et mystique chinoise.*
[2] ". . . The phenomenon produced by the contiguity of two surfaces of different colour or tone. Each plane of shade creates around itself a sort of aura of light, and each luminous plane creates around itself a zone of shade. In a similar way a coloured area communicates its 'complementary' to the neighbouring colour, or heightens it if it is 'complementary'."
[3] Signac, *op. cit.*

Towards 1885 the Impressionists (most of whom, incidentally, were to abandon their luminous palettes after 1890) were still painting "as birds sing". But they did not apply the law of simultaneous contrast logically, and sacrificed thoroughness to the "sensation" which was to fix the fleeting moment for all eternity. In fact, their application of the law of contrast was erratic, they often made mistakes, and in the end it was impossible to tell whether the fifteenth variant of some effect of sunlight had been painted at five o'clock in the morning or at seven in the evening.

Seurat and Signac set out to give method to Impressionism, and they were soon joined by Theo van Rysselberghe (1862–1926), who became Neo-Divisionism's portrait-painter, just as Renoir had for a while been Impressionism's portrait-painter. Henri-Edmond Cross (1856–1910), Dubois-Pillet, Angrand, Petitjean (1854–1926), Maximilien Luce (born in 1858), and others from all over the world joined Seurat and Signac.

Like the Impressionists, the Neo-Impressionists or Divisionists only used pure colours on their palettes but they rejected any mixing whatsoever except, of course, the fusion of adjacent colours on the canvas. "These colours, graded and lightened with white, were to correspond to the range of colours and tones in the solar spectrum. Orange, which could be graded towards yellow and red, violet which could pass from red to blue, green which could pass from blue to yellow, were, together with white, all they ever used. But, through fusing these few colours optically, and varying their proportions, they were able to obtain an infinite range, from the brightest to the greyest."[1]

In this way Divisionism was to assure "through the optical fusion of pure pigments, a maximum degree of luminosity and colour intensity; and, through the proportions and balance of these pigments according to the laws of contrast, of blending and radiation, the harmony of the picture as a whole."[2]

For, as Seurat declared to his biographer, Jean Christophe, "Art is harmony, and harmony is the analogy of *les contraires et les semblables*, in tone, colour and line. The colours are: red and its complementary, green; orange and its complementary, blue; yellow and its complementary, violet. . . . The means of expression is the optical fusion of

[1] Signac, *op. cit.*   [2] Signac, *op. cit.*

the tones and colours and their inter-action. (Shadows obey strict rules.)"

To achieve the general harmony of the picture, Divisionism co-ordinated the lines (directions and angles), the colours (hues) and the chiaroscuri (tones) according to the emotion the artist wanted to express. "Calm is expressed by the predominance of horizontal lines, joy by ascending lines, sorrow by descending lines. The intermediary lines represent all the other sensations in their infinite variety. The no less expressive and varied interplay of colours must correspond to the interplay of lines. Ascending lines need warm hues and light tones, descending lines must be predominantly in cold hues and dark tones, and a more or less perfect harmonising of warm and cold hues, of pale and vivid tones must reinforce the calm of horizontal lines."[1] Forestalling the criticism levelled against the Divisionist method, Signac declared that by "subordinating colour and line to the emotion which he feels and desires to express, the artist will achieve a poetical and creative work of art". And indeed, we are forced to admit that great masterpieces were painted in the past by artists who submitted to rules every bit as exacting as these.

Cézanne replaced the Impressionists' *comma* by a little dab which was like a living cell of paint. Vollard recalls how in Cézanne's portrait of him there was a tiny spot which was left bare. Cézanne was reluctant to paint it because he was afraid he would never guess the right tone and so would have to begin the picture afresh. Other pictures by Cézanne reveal similar blank spots which he doubtless intended to paint in as soon as he had discovered the right tone to use. One false tone would have dealt a death-blow to a picture to which he had given an organic life. But these blank spots were never covered in. (With the succeeding generation, it became fashionable to leave bare spots on the canvas, but this mannerism usually damaged the work of artists who practised it. Of one adept of this fashion, the Italian De Pisis, I wrote many years ago that one day his painting would consist of a bare canvas with nothing but his signature—this in any case already contained all the qualities of his plastic script.)

For the Impressionists' *comma* and Cézanne's *dab*, the Neo-Impressionists substituted what to the layman looks like a dot and which

[1] Signac, *op. cit.*

indeed is a dot. Naturally, we must not confuse the Divisionists with painters like Pissarro, who, out of all that complicated technique, only really understood and adopted the Divisionist method of *spotting* colour on to the canvas, and so turned the dot, which for Seurat, Signac, Van Rysselberghe and Cross was purely a *means*, into the *end* of their dreary painting.

But even Seurat's pictures were too spotty for Renoir, and he also objected that to see them properly he had to stand a certain distance away. "And I so love walking round a picture and picking it up in my hands", he complained to Vollard. "And what would you say if Veronese's *Last Supper* were painted in little dots?"

But we must not dwell any longer on Seurat as the originator of an æsthetic and technique which, like all æsthetics and techniques, has its defects and qualities. Obviously, if the Divisionists had painted vast murals instead of canvases, the fault to which Renoir objected would have been an asset. In any case, for Seurat, as for Signac in his early work, Divisionism was, perhaps unconsciously, a means, like the dot technique, rather than an end in itself.

As a matter of fact, I prefer Seurat's first great composition, *Un Dimanche à la Grande Jatte*, to his later works, such as *La Parade* and the unfinished *Le Cirque* (1891),[1] which "enabled painting to pass on to a lyrical plane".[2] But from a strictly Divisionist point of view *La Grande Jatte* is inferior even to *Les Poseuses* of 1888, a picture which infuriated Renoir.

To-day, as soon as we look at Seurat's drawings we see what great qualities he had as a colourist. They have been called the "finest drawings ever done by a painter". In these drawings he began by applying to chiaroscuro the theory of contrasts which he had discovered by analysing Delacroix and by studying Chevreul, Rood and Helmholtz on *le mélange optique*. No one could possibly have given a better description of Seurat's drawings than Lucie Cousturier (1871–1925), a writer and painter of remarkable talent: "The new and lasting beauty of these drawings", she wrote, "is due to the unlimited faith with which the artist entrusted the expression of his thoughts to the eloquence of contrasting blacks and whites. For example, in order

---

[1] Renoir called this picture "the last word in science".   [2] Ozenfant and Jeanneret, *op. cit.*

to convey the magnificence of a naked back, he did not stop to depict its muscles and undulating shape, he merely emphasised the luminous splendour of the flesh, either by enhancing the whites with sudden blacks or by toning them down, through delicate curves, to a powerful outline of shadow."

In his drawings, as in his paintings, Seurat stressed form, but not the form-light of the Impressionists.[1] Seurat's form emerges, as delicate as an apparition, from the contrasts of white and *condé* blacks. And it was in his form that the interplay of *vibrations colorées*, so dear to Laforgue, fused like blond fireworks.

Seurat's obsession with form became more and more pronounced as time passed, and finally he simply painted coloured poems which have a touch—I find it rather distasteful—of the picturesque, and a note of humour which is a little too familiar for my liking. But if we consider *La Baignade* (1884), *Un Dimanche à la Grande Jatte* (1886), *Les Poseuses* (1888) and the simpler pictures, we certainly understand why Seurat's "sober painting should have contributed as much as Cézanne's to the sensibility of someone like Picasso or Braque", as André Lhote put it in his essay *La Peinture*. It also affected Severini, whose influence, as we shall see, has been important in the evolution of modern art.

Seurat turned the Impressionists' "fleeting sensation" into a sort of lyrical architecture, and this, after the Impressionist carnival (Eugenio d'Ors must have coined this expression), reached, in *La Grande Jatte*, the gentle serenity of the old masters, "that serenity which prevents one from ever growing tired of looking at them, and which gives one the notion of eternity in art", as Renoir said. But Renoir was not conscious of the gentle serenity and deep enchantment of the first great masterpiece by Seurat, the great artist who tried in vain to make Impressionism eternal.

When we talk about Seurat it would be unfair not to mention

---

[1] As we have already seen, the Impressionists did indeed broach the problem of light and they solved it in terms of form: "Form from the æsthetic point of view and form from the purely pictorial point of view", as Severini put it. In this particular case it was the kind of form they required and it is foolish, therefore, to speak of the dissolution of form. However, with the Impressionists form was too bound up with the concept of light, and consequently it was inadequate for those who also set themselves other problems. This is why Seurat and, later, Delaunay, Léger and Severini felt the need to *intensify* Impressionism.

Signac's (1863–1935) first powerful harmonies—*Les Laveuses aux Andelys* (1886)—Van Rysselberghe's[1] *Portrait of the Poet Verhaeren*, Cross's mythological symphonies, Charles Angrand's pastels, and the works of Dubois-Pillet, an officer in the *Gardes Républicaines*, who was the first of the *peintres de dimanche*, a theoretician of Divisionism, and one of the founders of the *Salon des Indépendants*.

Though it may sound surprising at first, Impressionism was really the last serious attempt—made under the ægis of science—to establish naturalistic art. "If", said Signac, "it is any merit for an artistic method to resemble nature's system, let us point out that nature uses nothing but the colours of the solar spectrum, and does not allow a single square inch of smooth painting."

It may also sound strange if I say that Gauguin (1848–1903) and, to some extent, Van Gogh (1853–90) represented the anti-naturalist tendency of their time. But this was so. We need only remember what Cézanne wrote to Bernard in his famous letter on cylinders: "You will soon be turning your backs on painters like Gauguin and Van Gogh."

The painter Bernard met Gauguin at Pont-Aven in Brittany in 1886. Two years later, at the Bois d'Amour, Bernard introduced a fellow painter, Sérusier (1865–1927) to Gauguin, and from Gauguin both learnt of the existence of Cézanne and Van Gogh. Gauguin encouraged them not only "to paint what they saw", but to bring out, solidify and materialise in form and colour "*la pensée intime des choses et des êtres*", and he implored them to do away with chiaroscuro and *trompe l'œil*, a pet device of the painter Gérome, as being subterfuges unworthy of an artist. "The only thing permissible is the noble arabesque which enables the sensibility to follow its capricious labyrinths right to the heart. In art, every means is good. Nature can be violated and brought back to permanent beauty through sublime contortion."[2]

Thus, side by side with Symbolism in literature—Gauguin was a friend of Verlaine and Mallarmé—developed Symbolism in painting. Round the Pont-Aven school and the *Nabis* this Symbolist movement united traditionalist painters, painters who had remained faithful to

---

[1] Van Rysselberghe was the only Divisionist who was ever commissioned to do vast mural decorations. These are to be found in Neuilly and Brussels.

[2] Gauguin, *Noa-Noa* and other writings.

the smooth tradition, and refugees from Impressionism such as Sérusier, Seguin, Laval, and Maufra. Later on it was joined by artists who were to attain truer and better deserved fame, such as Maillol, Vuillard, Redon, Denis and Bonnard.

For Gauguin, as for Mallarmé, *"un coup de dé jamais n'abolira le hasard"*, because a picture, like a poem, is *"un coup de dé pour arriver à une combinaison éternelle"*.[1]

Like Seurat, Gauguin sought harmony, but Gauguin rejected contrasts. He did not believe in perfecting things too much: "the impression is so short-lived that if one then elaborates the details too late one runs the risk of ruining the initial freshness or immediacy of a work of art". But above all, he said, "see that everything lives in the higher calm of the spirit. Avoid the moment. Let your figures be static". And again: "The laws of beauty certainly do not lie in the truths of nature. They must be sought elsewhere."

But Gauguin's Symbolism was not at all like Puvis de Chavanne's. "Puvis", wrote Gauguin, "would give the title *Purity* to a picture of a virgin girl with a lily." But for Gauguin *purity* would be represented by a landscape with an expanse of limpid water, and with not a single trace of man; or perhaps, at most, one figure.

Gauguin could not renounce nature, and indeed, nature was his essential ideal, but he wanted virgin nature, uncontaminated by man. And he did not seek nature with his eyes, like the Impressionists, but through his soul. It was in exile, in Tahiti and the Marquesas that he discovered nature, *belle comme l'extase*, "fabulous colours everywhere, air like fire, but pure and tranquil in its silence".[2]

Symbolism, or Neo-Traditionalism, as it was called by Maurice Denis, who was twenty years old in 1890, was to be the "universal triumph of æsthetic imagination over stupid imitation of nature" and "the triumph of beauty over the naturalist lie". Art, therefore, should be emotional as it was with Gauguin, who was above all a poet.

And, indeed, Symbolism was characterised by emotional inwardness and a vague yearning for ecstasy which in Gauguin was barbarous, in a certain sense, and recalled Verlaine:

[1] B. Fay, *Panorama de la Littérature Contemporaine.*   [2] Gauguin, *op. cit.*

"Je suis l'Empire à la fin de la décadence
Qui regarde passer les grands Barbares blancs
En composant des acrostiches indolents
D'un style d'or où la langueur du soleil danse."

The Symbolists retained their characteristics after the dispersal of the group—which, by the way, was short-lived—and even after they had abandoned the doctrines they once proclaimed with so much confidence. Their one undeniable victory was in the field of theatrical decoration. "Under Paul Fort's and Lugné-Poe's leadership, Bonnard, Denis, Ranson, K. X. Roussel, Odilon Redon, Sérusier, and Vuillard courageously fought against Antoine's flat naturalism and against the childish stage tricks of the *Théatre Libre*. Indeed, to them we owe the principles which have reformed stage decoration."[1]

Odilon Redon, who wavered between mysterious virginal profiles and realistic bunches of flowers, Sérusier (1865–1927), who later discovered Cézanne's geometrics, and Maurice Denis, whose Christian ecstasies never attained the magnificence of Gauguin's pagan ecstasies, were the only three artists who could still claim the title "Symbolists". The chief distinction of Maurice Denis (born 1870) was that he painted an *Hommage à Cézanne* after a visit to Aix. In this picture the Symbolist painters, Odilon Redon, Vuillard, Mellerio, Maurice Denis, Ranson, Roussel, Bonnard, as well as Vollard and Mme Denis, are grouped round a still life by Cézanne—the famous *Compotier*—listening, pale with tension, to Sérusier's explanations. This was the first tribute paid to Cézanne, the hermit of Aix. The Symbolism of the work lies entirely in the subject. The Neo-Traditionalists recognise that emotion in painting must be exclusively plastic and they bow in reverence to Cézanne, the artist who was a painter even before he began to paint, and even before he became an artist.

But such symbolical language does not appear to have been understood by all the former Symbolists. Vuillard (1868–1940), for example, cannot be said to have grasped it, though his work has the soulful inwardness of Symbolism and he applied the Impressionist *comma* technique in a gloomy way. At the outbreak of the late war, Vuillard was the favourite of a certain section of the French bourgeoisie—the

[1] R. Escholier, *La Peinture au XXème Siècle*.

deux cent familles who were apparently responsible for the collapse of 1940—but the only thing he got from Cézanne was the patent of nobility Cézanne conferred on wall-paper.[1] This was sufficient to turn Vuillard into "*Le Petit Maître du papier peint, des dessus de piano et des affreux abat-jour à volants*", as my intelligent collaborator, Pierre Guéguen, aptly put it in the *XXème Siècle*.

Like Vuillard, Bonnard (1867–1947) remained faithful to the inwardness he inherited from Symbolism, but Bonnard turned this inwardness into a quivering and sensual ecstasy of pure colours, a festival of light. His sensibility, like Gauguin's, reaches the heart through a capricious labyrinth, and when one looks at his most recent works one cannot help being reminded of Mallarmé, especially of *Les Divagations.* "I have always had a passion for solitude", said Bonnard. "How many long days have I spent alone with my cat, and when I say *alone*, I mean without a material being, for my cat is a mystical companion, a spirit. . . . And my favourite days in the year are the last languid days of summer, the ones immediately preceding autumn. And the hour of the day when I love to walk is the hour when the sun rests, just before disappearing, with its yellow-copper rays on grey walls and its red-copper rays on bricks." Like Picasso, Pierre Bonnard began by undergoing the influence of Toulouse-Lautrec (at the time when, like Picasso, and later than Van Gogh, he was perhaps attracted by social art), then was a convert to Impressionism, and to Symbolism, and finally became known for the sensuality of his scenes of Paris. This was observable before he began to specialise, like Degas —but without that misogynist's crudeness and indeed with a rustic and healthy sweetness—in the secrets of women's toilet. His colours were already warm and thick. The thickness remained, but the warmth became heat, and finally light. At one time it looked as though he realised how far his obsession with colour had taken him: "Almost

---

[1] "Wall-paper, with its geometrical patterns and ornamental flowers which he [Cézanne] incorporates into the rhythm of line and colour, is one of the realistic elements peculiar to Cézanne's world. These he used admirably, either by paraphrasing them, or by making them serve to prolong or accentuate a certain flow of lines or a certain note of colour. For example, in the same picture (*La Léçon de Piano*) the flower pattern in the background is picked up again in the armchair cover which certainly does not find itself in the foreground by chance. Such fundamental rhythmical elements are to be found in the best painters, but perhaps we should have taken longer to become aware of them, had it not been for Cézanne, for the academies and art schools would certainly not have drawn our attention to them" (Severini, "Cézanne", *Emporium*, October, 1936).

unconsciously I have sacrificed form to colour. But it is true that form exists and that one can adapt and transform it arbitrarily and endlessly. Therefore it is drawing that I must study. At present I am drawing incessantly. And after drawing, I must try to balance my composition." "*A well composed picture is a picture half finished*", he said to Terrasse. But colour triumphed. It is sensual not because it can be felt with the senses, but because the emotion which it communicates to the spirit seems to expand afterwards and overflow even into the senses. Another reason why it is called sensual is in order to distinguish it from Matisse's way of feeling colour which is exquisitely cerebral. The kind of emotion I am describing is a pure emotion, as I have already explained in connection with Renoir's sensuality. Yet Bonnard's painting—or, rather, his colour—does not merely create a visible universe; it also gives it a flavour and a scent. "Painting", said Gauguin, "is the most expressive of the arts. It can convey the most dissimilar emotions. It is a complete art which absorbs all the others and integrates them."[1]

But this had to be proved.

It is not that Bonnard's work, being more complete, is consequently superior to the painting, for example, of Matisse. Baudelaire is more complete than Goethe, but, although Baudelaire is a great poet, we cannot compare him with the author of *Faust*. Certainly Bonnard is the only artist to-day who fulfils Gauguin's definition in *Noa-Noa*.

[1] Gauguin, *op. cit.*

No False Modesty

IN the last three chapters I gave scarcely more than an indication of the important role cafés played in the life of artists from the second half of the last century to the end of the 1914–18 War. Cafés were also very important in the literary life of the same period, if less so than for artists. Literary men lived in cafés like champion exhibits of the human race, but painters lived in cafés as though cafés were academies. When they had lost all confidence in the teaching of the academies, they gathered in cafés to listen to Manet, who reigned at the *Guerbois*, to Monet and Pissarro, and as time went on, to Gauguin, Sérusier, Maurice Denis, Signac, Matisse, Picasso, Severini[1] and Gris. From Montmartre to Montparnasse, from the *Lapin Agile* to the *Closerie de Lilas*, from the right to the left bank of the Seine—which separates the heraldic area of the city into two camps and is the stem, rather than the cradle, of modern art—from the *Guerbois* to the *Dome* and to the *Rotonde*, painters eagerly awaited a Promethean spark which would set alive their closed horizons of clay. After the disastrous armistice of 1918, cafés became zoological gardens for artists too, and they now sat there complacently like poets, to be viewed with admiration or contempt by the crowd. But between 1860 and 1920, except in the case of Degas and Toulouse-Lautrec, who only went to them in order to find subjects for their caricatures, cafés were almost the baptismal fonts of modern art. Impressionism, Divisionism and Symbolism were born in cafés. Gertrude Stein would like it to be said that Fauvism and Cubism— of which the authoress of *The Making of Americans* claimed to be the godmother though in fact she was only a witness and a witness of no excessive interest, as we can see when we read her clever but burlesque *Autobiography of Alice B. Toklas*—were born in her little abode in the rue de Fleurus. But in the writings of Apollinaire, the real godfather

---

[1] Picasso, Severini and Marcoussis used to go to the *Brasserie de l'Hermitage*, in the Boulevard Rochechouard. Picasso could not bear overcrowded meetings, and one evening, so as to shake himself free from a boring group of Germans, he fired a revolver into the air.

of Cubism, and in André Salmon's memoirs, cafés play a much bigger part than the great and irrepressible Gertrude Stein. She was never able to achieve full friendship with either Matisse or Picasso, and only seems to have done so with Juan Gris, the last of the Cubists, because his death prevented the quarrel inevitable in her friendships.

Were the division of art into terms of centuries not purely arbitrary, we could say that while Fauvism marks the end of the art of the nineteenth century, a long-drawn-out end like a northern sunset, Cubism is the dawn of the art of our century, with all the colouring and huge promises of dawn.

In contrast with the tendencies preceding it and with those which were to follow, Fauvism was neither a technique nor an æsthetic system. The term *Fauvism* originated with a phrase of an art critic Louis Vauxelles. When he once saw a statuette exhibited in the room secured in the *Salon d'Automne* of 1905 by students of the Atelier Gustave Moreau and their friends, he exclaimed: "*Voici Donatello au milieu des fauves*" and his definition was accepted by the artists themselves. For most of them, for Braque, Derain, Vlaminck, Van Dongen and many others, Fauvism was no more than an incident in their evolution, an important incident, a stage but nothing more. For Matisse, Marquet, Rouault, Dufy and Friesz it was no more than a point of departure. Rouault has hardly ever moved from it since, Marquet and Friesz tended to lose sight of it, and Matisse and Dufy can recall it with an element of satisfaction when they look back on the road they have happily travelled, through dangers of every kind, each according to his own capacity.

But for all alike Fauvism meant above all the discovery of the Mediterranean. In the name of the Mediterranean, it floated a youthful and noisy reaction, not, as is usually said, against Impressionism but against the technique of the Impressionists. In preference to simultaneous contrasts, the Fauves went in for the so-called contrasts of mass with their wider and more sonorous orchestration; but they respected all the other achievements of Impressionism and Neo-Impressionism.

In 1897, when he was twenty-eight years old, Henri Matisse (born at Cateau in 1869) painted the *Desserte*, now in the Freudenberg Collection. This picture, involving a modern application of Chardin's technique, might have justified Matisse had he claimed that he had now discovered his way. Anyone else, according to Roger Fry, would certainly have done so. But Matisse had the courage to abandon a system which assured him of success and a brilliant position. The same thing happened a few years later in the case of Picasso. With the harlequins of his blue period and the adolescents of his rose period, he too had already achieved enough to establish his fame as an artist. And Renoir, too, abandoned the easy way of Impressionism, though he was among its greatest masters, because he felt the need to solve his own problem. But whereas Renoir's problem was that of a reconciliation with tradition, Matisse's problem was entirely different, almost the opposite.

For a while Signac was able to interest Matisse in Divisionism. This was a new success. Matisse painted *Luxe, Calme, Volupté* (1904), and the Divisionists thought they had found a new leader. But Divisionism did not solve Matisse's problem. He abandoned Seurat's æsthetics and adopted the attitude of the Fauves.

But what did this attitude consist in? According to René Huyghe, "the Fauves are out for conciseness because what they want to achieve above all else is intensity". But I have already said that the key to Fauvism, or to Matisse, lies in the discovery of the Mediterranean. And the Mediterranean, which in French painting now only makes us think of Matisse, was already to be found in Cézanne (conciseness) and Van Gogh (intensity). Between these two great isolated figures there was Gauguin, the Symbolist, who seemed to have discovered a middle way between east and west and to have struck the balance—between conciseness and intensity—demanded by his subject. This was because Gauguin, as creator of *Hina te Fatou* (The Moon and the Earth), felt that painting, like literature, "involves a story", but has the additional advantage that "the reader can embrace the whole development at once".

Matisse was quite right in thinking that no one interpreted nature with greater intensity than Van Gogh (1853–90). But he was of the opinion that Van Gogh lacked real plastic education—in other words, had no real technique. For all his genius, Vincent Van Gogh painted like a self-taught man. But for a short time Matisse was seduced by

Van Gogh's juxtapositions. Van Gogh himself confessed: "I beat on the canvas with irregular blows and leave them as they stand." And again: "Daubs, bare pieces of canvas here and there, corners left entirely unfinished, fresh starts, new efforts and brutalities. And the result, I am beginning to think, is altogether too disquietening and tiresome to make for the happiness of people who have their own ideas about technique." When he was not hammering and daubing, Van Gogh spread colour on to the canvas in tufts, or rather in tongues of fire (like the ones on the famous tabernacle described by Manzoni) going upwards, or curled in on themselves when they represented burning suns, with haloes like the haloes round the hosts in the holy pictures he must have seen in the hands of little boys in Arles.

Van Gogh's brutality, which is also his intensity, must have inflamed sensations Matisse already felt. The Fauve Matisse wanted to roar, and never did an artist's brush roar more powerfully than Van Gogh's. But Matisse and Gauguin were brought together by their literary education and by the admiration both felt for Mallarmé. Moreover, Matisse could not be indifferent to Gauguin's musical conception of painting nor to the revolutionary way in which he transformed the plastic values of traditional painting into a pattern of zones of pure colour. Cézanne seemed less Mediterranean when seen from Collioure rather than Paris, and this too was a useful indication. For it cannot have escaped Matisse that whereas Van Gogh's form was a dramatic deformation of nature, and that of Gauguin was inscribed within the limits of a decadent idealism and bordered on a vague kind of primitivism, the form attained by Cézanne between 1880 and 1895 involved a logical transformation or transfiguration of nature.

So Matisse absorbed all the plastic experiments which had been made since Delacroix. It has been said, perhaps a little too hastily, that he abolished the subject in painting. What in fact he did do was to carry the subject to the extreme limits of transfiguration. He brought a whole period in the history of art to a happy conclusion—he did not attempt, like Picasso, to open a new epoch. At present we are only examining the beginnings of this conclusion. In his Fauve version of the *Desserte*, and in *Joie de Vivre*, which won him the position of leader of the Fauves—for this reason we now see him as embodying the whole of Fauvism—Matisse doubtless did abandon himself too easily to the joy of movement and arabesque voluptuousness, and even came dangerously close to the "ornamental". Through his introduction of movement, Matisse took up a position contrary to the static conception of painting held by his three great predecessors. There was an arabesque element already in Cézanne's painting, though it was more hinted at than expressed. With Matisse it became a dynamic rhythm, a raging and delirious frenzy.

No one has ever pointed out the measure of correspondence between Matisse's Fauvism and Cézanne's romantic period. What I mean is that for an artist who had already produced works so happily balanced as the first *Desserte*, Fauvism came above all as a wild intoxication, as though for a time Matisse felt an urge to destroy the romantic inheritance, of which a part had also fallen to him.

Later on, when he visited Morocco for a short time, Matisse veered towards Cubism and perceived the importance it conferred on the object "as a classical pretext and a means of plastic evocation".[1] But this phase was only momentary, and Cubism must have seemed to him far too steeped in scientific theories. Matisse, like Cézanne, could not bear people who "only see dead geometry, anatomy or perspective in a picture and therefore exclude every living quality from bodies and content themselves with mechanical frameworks expressing space, and material dimensions, but not the vibrations of the spirit", to quote the Italian Carrà. Cubism was not really like this, but it must have appeared so to Matisse, whose destiny it was to bring one epoch to a conclusion, but not to become the voluntary beginner of another. We must do Matisse the justice too of recognising that he has never accepted a ready-made solution, but has always sought for it through his own experience. If Matisse turned to Cubism for a time, it was because it was part of his natural development to do so.[2]

---

[1] Christian Zervos, *Cahiers d'Art.*

[2] In 1917 (Matisse had already spent several successive winters in Morocco) he saw a great deal of the Cubists and they went to see him at Clamart or at 19 Quai St. Michel. This was a period of great discussions and Raymond Escholier did not fail to notice in Matisse's work of that time a sort of "geometrical *parti-pris* and a Constructivist will" which revealed a certain influence of Cubist doctrines.
Indeed, one day Matisse showed me a sketch he had made in a street in Tangiers. In the foreground there was a wall painted in blue which dominated the whole of the picture. Matisse gave it the maximum importance possible while yet preserving the objective construction of the scene. In

From *Joie de Vivre* up to his latest paintings, the direction Matisse followed was parallel, though on a different plane, to the one followed by Cézanne from the time of his first romantic compositions until—for example—the *Portrait de Vollard*. Matisse had, that is, the same intention to dominate the plastic life of painting, to control sensations and to exclude any emotion contrary to reason. In all this, like Cézanne, he had discipline without scientific puritanism—a picture is above all an *œuvre du cœur*; it is love and not science.

I am almost painfully surprised that Pierre Courthion, one of the ablest art critics of our time and an old and close friend of mine, should have said in his recent book on Matisse which is otherwise so commendable: "I almost resent him for his confidence in his use of tones, because he knows too well what he is doing. Romantic sentiment—that dark rose of our human instability—is almost lacking in him. I should like to see this sentiment more expressed (just as sometimes I should have liked to have seen Mallarmé come down to earth). Icarus only moves us because he fell." This surprises me because it suggests that Matisse wished above all to impress spectators by his confidence, whereas the truth is just the opposite. A recent picture by Matisse gives the same impression of joy and spontaneity as the best successes of his Fauve period. The only difference is that his recent paintings are constructed, so to speak, for eternity.[1] There is spite of this, he confessed that he had not reproduced even the hundredth part of the sensory intensity aroused in him by that blue.

He reached this level of intensity in another picture, *Les Marocains*, but here the actual architecture of the landscape was replaced by an architecture which was Constructivist, and yet "felt". By using sensation as a constituent element in the work, but not as its only *raison d'être* or point of departure, Matisse, with the help of Cubist theories, rediscovered the architectonic and free spirit characteristic of the Byzantines. (The Cubists knew Byzantine work.) And his colour became increasingly spiritual and abstract, almost independent of the objects or reality on which it was used; the latter for him were secondary (Severini, *Matisse*, Rome, 1944).

To the experiments of the Cubists Matisse added the *object*, whose plastic virginity, so to speak, Cézanne had already indicated. The object, hitherto kept in the shade by the great masters, almost as though it were a poor relation, had had to be contented with the affection of Chardin and a few Dutch *petits maîtres*. Cézanne painted a still life with as much, or even greater, care than he used in painting a portrait. But in his early works Matisse actually humiliated living bodies and exalted objects with "the proud insolence of instinct" (Zervos). For him, therefore, just as for the Cubists a few years later, the object was a pretext for giving free rein to imagination and plastic poetry.

[1] "Matisse's work has acquired greater order, sumptuousness and plastic perfection, but it has not surpassed the incisive style of his youthful work. One sees this clearly from his colours. In his youth Matisse was at great pains to discover all the secrets of colour. For this purpose he made the most complicated experiments and obtained sensational results. But there remained the problem of atmosphere. It is only in the last few years and after long and assiduous efforts that he has managed to situate the object in atmosphere and to outline it in space. To-day he is the absolute master of colour; he has discovered the most subtle relations of tones, and their most intimate and crystalline fusions" (Zervos, *Cahiers d'Art*).

no ground for complaint because Matisse, like Cézanne, has returned to static forms—which are incidentally better in keeping with his conception of painting as a two-dimensional rather than a three-dimensional art. We must not forget that one of the first results of the revolution started by Delacroix was to compel artists to go back, as I said earlier on, beyond the Italian origins of painting to its Byzantine fountain-head. Matisse does believe in theories up to a point. He said to Tériade that the first studies of a picture have no other purpose than to prepare the soul and to "*nourrir le sentiment*".

Like Roger Fry, who wrote on Matisse for my review, the Italian critic Gino Visentini[1] is of the opinion that "Matisse sees nature and man as though they were objects or a tapestry. In fact, he reduces everything to tapestry". But it would be wrong to take this observation in a derogatory sense. If a painting by Matisse makes Roger Fry and Visentini think of tapestry, it is because tapestry, in its best periods, is an art expressing itself in two dimensions, whereas painting endeavoured to convey, not only the colour of an object, but the substance of which it is composed—in other words, "the delicate vitality of flesh, the softness of fabrics, the delicacy of flowers, the succulence of fruit", etc. This was a quality praised by Baldassare Castiglione as "adding solemnity to a work of art, and in a certain sense divinity, as though the work were brought to perfection like a work of God",[2] a quality which "consists in using a kind of indifference which disguises the artificial". But tapestry, faithful to the concept of pure depiction, fulfilled the instinct which "makes us see the world as a *woven tissue* of tones, masses and values rhythmically distributed". It was Manet, as we have seen, who reintroduced this instinct into modern painting, and it has continued to flourish save in the striking case of Renoir, who was able to prove that one can be modern and yet allow colours to express the "delicate vitality of flesh". But though Matisse, true to Delacroix's teaching, is not afraid to paint the nudes of his odalisques, if not with mud itself, at least in grey, a colour no less distasteful to the painters of recent generations, his pictures are shrill with chromatic intensity. "When I use a green", he said to Courthion, "I don't pretend that it is grass, and when I use a blue, I don't think

[1] In *Gusti Esagerati*.   [2] U. Ojetti, *Ottocento, Novecento e via dicendo*.

of it as the colour of the sky." But he does not use blue or red indifferently, like Picasso. To find just the right blue, he is capable of going all round the world.[1] In Africa, Italy and Tahiti, he did nothing but look for a blue, a green and a red. Gertrude Stein said that the enthusiasm displayed by Matisse's first wife during their travels in Italy was not at all shared by Matisse, who, doubtless, finds all sentimental turmoil stupid. During the summer of the Munich "war of nerves", I used to meet Matisse almost every evening after dinner, and we used to sit and talk at a table in a milk-bar at Montparnasse until it was late enough to go to bed. The only thing Matisse remembered about Tahiti was the illegitimate children French writers and officials had left there, and the disappointment of his models when they discovered, after posing for him, that he did not share the appetites which they were accustomed to satisfy in other painters. And then, too, he recalled a certain sunset when he had seen an extraordinary and unexpected harmony of colours reflected in a mirror, or he would remember some object or other he had enjoyed painting. But when I asked him what impression the scenery had made on him, he immediately replied that a flower had given him the idea for a piece of sculpture (Matisse is also a great sculptor)—the head he allowed me to photograph and reproduce on the cover of the Christmas Number of *XXème Siècle*. But he said that he did not like being reminded of it, because his own work never gave him any of the childish pride which binds a father to his son, the creator to his creation. He could look on his own work as though it had been done by someone else. The only benefit he got out of travelling was the fund of memories it provided.

René Huyghe, who has written what is considered the final word on Matisse's colour, says: "Matisse's extraordinary achievement is due to the fact that he offers the spectator nothing but living colour sensations and never imposes on him the burden of boredom and satiety."

[1] To Tériade, however, he expressed almost identically the same view as Picasso held—namely, that a black can easily be used instead of a blue because at bottom the final expression is due to the relations of tones. One is not a slave to a blue, or a green or a red. The relations can be altered by varying the quantity of the elements of their nature. In other words, a picture will always be painted with a blue, a yellow and a green of which the proportions can be varied. Or the relations constituting the expression of a picture can be designated by substituting a black for a blue, just as in an orchestra one can substitute an oboe for a small trumpet. But when he painted *La Danse*, which is now in the Barnes Foundation at Philadelphia, Matisse waited for a certain blue needed by the harmony of the picture to be specially prepared for him by a German factory of chemical products. And he wanted me to use the very blue he had used in painting the picture for a reproduction which I once arranged.

He suggests that Matisse reached this miraculous result by alternating sensations of colour with sensations of colourlessness; in other words, by creating "an area of rest" beside "an area of sensation". "A colour remains fresh on black or on white because the sensation of coloured light is alternated with a sensation of colourlessness." But obviously the secret of Matisse's painting cannot lie in this alone. Columbus's egg does not explain the discovery of America. I remember how Renoir, when he was paralysed, used to model masterpieces through the hands of a professional sculptor. No one could have known Renoir's secret better than this man; but after Renoir's death he was incapable of making a single bronze worthy of being placed on a mantelpiece.

It is impossible to discover Matisse's secret even when we know that it was only after long, analytical researches that he arrived at his synthesis and carried it to its purest expression. For Matisse hides nothing in his art. He has no false modesty. If he had had any false modesty, he would not have been a Fauve. He does not even hide any of his hesitations. And it is easy to see on his canvases, as on Manet's, the old outline hardly effaced beside the new one.

Mallarmé's name has been mentioned in connection with Matisse. But Mallarmé set out from a simple idea or a simple sensation, often from both at once, and arrived at a total complex of ideas and sensations. With Matisse it is the opposite, and that is why the author of *L'Après-midi d'un Faune* and the painters of the *Odalisques* round off the circle between them, whereas Bonnard is only Mallarmé's plastic counterpart.

From a purely revolutionary point of view, Matisse took liberties with form which no one before him would have dared to do. "With Matisse", wrote Ozenfant and Jeanneret, "lyricism acquired the right to take every possible liberty. Braque and Picasso were to break the last chains of art." But though Matisse's work brought nineteenth-century art to a close with a brilliant sunset, this does not prevent his work from being more full of valuable hints, and more fertile, than that of the actual innovators of the twentieth century. On several occasions, towards 1930 and again in 1938, Picasso relished Matisse with even more enjoyment than he got from Ingres after his Cubist-Abstract period. Perhaps it would be worth adding that Matisse had the ability to *invent* his own colours but he never managed to give them a new form and did no more than take liberties with the colours he inherited from Manet. But this, be it understood, is only an observation, it isn't a reproof.

Although it may be true that the very latest Matisse has no direct and certain forerunners, it is impossible to agree with Courthion's claim that Matisse is the most isolated artist of contemporary painting. At present a whole group of young artists looks towards him, and it would appear that recent developments among young French painters involve a decision to return to Fauvism. These returns are never barren,[1] and it is to be hoped that Léon Gischia, for example, will soon be able to produce something in relation to Matisse, which will be what *Joie de Vivre* was in relation to Cézanne, Van Gogh, and Gauguin.

One need only think of Raoul Dufy (born at Le Havre in 1877), on whom Courthion has published an excellent monograph—he has since doubtless forgotten it—to see that Matisse was never an *Isolé*. Dufy's inspiration, as he himself points out, sprang from a painting by Matisse, *Luxe, Calme, Volupté*. But *Joie de Vivre* impressed him even more deeply. Dufy was won over by the vitality of Matisse's colouring and by the animation of certain "calligraphic mouldings", as they have been called by Giorgio Castelfranco (who thinks he can be enthusiastic about modern art without including Matisse—just as though we were to admire nineteenth-century French painting without giving his due to Delacroix). As a matter of fact, Dufy expresses, even more vigorously than Matisse, the *joie de vivre* which French painting has in vain been trying to give to the world. Moreover, we admire not only his most recent works, in which he has achieved a personal and almost translucent kind of writing; we also admire his work which dates from the time when, after the intoxication of the Fauves, he was among the first, together with Picasso, Derain and Braque, to sense the advent of Cubism.

[1] "When methods have become so refined and so subtle that they have exhausted their powers of expression, one must return to the essential principles which have formed the human language. It is then the principles themselves which live again, and reanimate us and give us a new lease of life" (Matisse, to Tériade).

One must not look upon these returns as being movements intended to bring back to life old art conceptions which can at most give birth to still-born work. This was Kandinsky's warning in his famous book on *Spirituality in Art*. A fruitful revival can only be a point of contact which, "by exalting the creative faculty of the artist, will enable him to throw new light into the depths of the human heart".

47

In those days he used to light up the centre of his pictures, leaving the sides in the shade, and, like Cézanne, he used to draw as he painted. To-day he is primarily concerned with colour arrangement, as though the visible world were above all a feast of colours, and he translates into pure colour the light which enters the picture from the two sides. The centre of the picture is left to create a "zone of rest", as it has been called, and it separates into two parts, with a clear division, the objects which are, as it were, arranged on its boundaries, and with which he then covers his canvas, using the tip of his brush and painting as though he were writing, but writing transparently. Thus the objects are half illuminated and half in darkness, and follow a discipline which is in no sense naturalistic—exactly as in some of Braque's pictures. René Huyghe maintains that Matisse's black gives a colourless sensation which rests the eye from the sensation of colour produced by yellow, for example; but in Dufy's painting blacks themselves are still full of light and, as Christian Zervos says, *"ils situent avec précision les bleus des paysages méditerranéens"*. In *Hommage à Claude Lorrain*, the picture in which Dufy first discovered lateral lighting, "black becomes the dominant colour of the picture". To think that the Impressionists tried to banish it from their palettes! With Dufy, black returned to reign over the other colours, and made, so to speak, "the colour relations of the painting".

If Dufy's technique makes us think of etching, the technique of Georges Rouault (born 1871), a fellow pupil of Matisse in the *Atelier Gustave Moreau*, seems to derive from Gothic stained-glass work. And it is not only his technique which is Gothic. "A friend of Léon Bloy and of J. K. Huysmans, he too went on a pilgrimage to the monastery of Ligugé, where the author of *Là-Bas* hoped to found a sort of sodality of Catholic artists. At that time Rouault was painting imaginary landscapes, in nocturnal blues, dotted about with unreal and scintillating lights. Then, towards 1903, he discovered the circus, and examined with growing emotion all its tricks of deception. He discovered, above all, the misery hidden under the paint on the grotesque faces of clowns. All this afforded the colourist with endless opportunities for bringing together vehement, stridently sonorous colours, and for bursting out into blood-red lacquers, sulphurous

48

yellows, poisonous Prussian blues, emerald greens and for using black, *l'agent de l'esprit*, as Vigny called it. Apart from the great painter Daumier, no one ever felt so much human sympathy for the secret life of the circus world, a life so despised and overlooked, so wonderful to anyone who has been able to get near it and understand it."[1]

A little later Rouault's fiery spirit vented itself freely upon those called *les filles*. "Never was prostitution flagellated with more indignation and fury, not even by the author of *Les Caprices*, nor by Degas, nor even by Toulouse-Lautrec himself", observes Raymond Escholier. After *les filles*, he turned on lawyers and judges. Finally, when he had quenched his burning thirst for justice, Rouault took refuge in faith, and henceforth his work was dedicated to religious subjects. "In his religious scenes and his portraits of Christ there is a sort of Byzantine echo, a great breath of pathos coming from Colmar and Grünewald's *Calvary*. Georges Rouault may well be the greatest Catholic artist of our time."[2]

I have said that Rouault's technique makes us think of the stained-glass painting of the great Gothic cathedrals. The figures are not merely drawn; they are hemmed in by thick contours within which the medley of colours glitters like a jewel.

Vollard attempted to secure all Rouault's work, just as he was interested for many years in the experiments of Picasso, Vlaminck, Derain and Matisse. But one day Matisse waited for him in vain in his studio, and was about to give up painting and take up a post in the municipality, to save his children from starvation, when he was rescued by a Russian Jew whose collection of pictures now forms the *Moscow Museum of Western Art*. Rouault was the only one who let himself be caught, *qui se laissa mettre le grappin dessus*, as Cézanne used to say. Rouault has now shut himself up for many years in a curious language of his own and manages to talk as only Mallarmé could write, and maintains that he has suffered under the tutelage of Cézanne's dealer. But if this suffering has influenced his work in any way, then I think he ought to thank Heaven for having brought it about.

André Derain (born 1880) has classical and Latin leanings, and for

[1] R. Escholier, *op. cit.*   [2] Ibid.

this reason in recent years he has lost some of his admirers in France, and has been accused of betraying the ideals of the new French painting; and he has lost ground in Italy too, for there people are unwilling to take lessons from foreigners in matters of Classicism and Latinity. Towards 1919 the Italian painter Carrà heralded Derain as the Gothic-Flemish counterpart of the Mediterranean Matisse. It was only after 1920, during a journey in Italy to visit the places where the art of Claude Lorrain and Nicolas Poussin was begotten, that Derain felt the irresistible call of Classicism, and it is not impossible that, like Renoir, for whom the discovery of Italy proved fatal for some years, he may yet return to the aspirations of his early youth. From 1908 up to the present day Derain has felt the appeal of all the epochs of French painting, from the Primitives to the Romantics, to Cézanne and Renoir—though in the way in which it can only be experienced by one of the most cultured men of our time who happens also to be endowed with great feeling for painting. The attitude of certain young men to-day to Derain is all the more shocking and presumptuous, since the tiniest fraction of his work is often worth more than their whole output set together.

But it is almost impossible to speak of Derain without first paying tribute to Maurice de Vlaminck (born 1877), the founder of what André Salmon jokingly calls *l'école de l'école de Chatou*. Vlaminck won his first laurels as a cyclist; then, it appears, invented a sort of pre-Fauvism and discovered the Negro art which Matisse was later to reveal to Picasso, as Gertrude Stein tells us in the autobiography of her secretary, to which we have already referred. Certainly he was one of the first to undergo the influence of Van Gogh, who later became so important among the Fauves. A great talker and pamphleteer, though in this latter capacity he is unfortunate and even repellent, Vlaminck in his circle of friends has always been the one who explains everything, *qui explique le coup*, as André Salmon puts it. He teaches the lesson rather like Pissarro, and like Pissarro he sowed and reaped as long as he was *en possession de ses moyens*. But for the last thirty years or so he has been painting almost nothing but the dramatic landscapes of the banks of the Seine or the Oise, or vases of flowers and still-lifes with nothing but Prussian blues and emerald greens.

The first influence Derain underwent was that of Vlaminck at Chatou, but immediately afterwards he met Matisse and became temporarily his pupil. Derain was amongst the most scandalous participants at the exhibition of the Fauves in 1905, for at Collioure Matisse had revealed to him the intensity of Mediterranean light. Matisse was then thirty-five years old and Derain twenty-four.

Just as Vlaminck's first paintings were a forecast of Fauvism, so some of Derain's landscapes (by this time he had met Picasso at Cadaquès in Catalonia during the summer holidays) heralded Cubism. Negro art and Cézanne predominated over this first period, but Derain did not follow Picasso in the adventurous quest for an abstract art.

Derain's Gothic period, undoubtedly his most evenly successful period, began in 1912 and was interrupted by the war—for, being a simple soldier, he never got a single day to himself. To this period belong *La Cène*, *Le Samedi*, in the Moscow Museum, *Les Buveurs*, *Les Deux Sœurs*, *Le Portrait du Chevalier X*, a few landscapes in which some people have recognised the happy influence of Giotto and the Byzantines while others, like Pierre Courthion, see in them the power and sonority of Poussin. At that time Derain represented, as Carrà rightly remarked, "a very plausible protest against the intoxication of colour", since he preferred warm and restful colours to strident ones, and was "the most assiduous explorer of iron greys".[1]

But after his journey in Italy his colour became more compact and his texture thicker. His forms became more rounded and were imbued with the Classical spirit which, though derived from museums, was corrected by his lively modern temperament. He sought for and found in museums the inspiration Corot looked for in nature. Here and there a rough sketch still recalls the early Derain. His best nudes date from this period, as well as his famous portraits of *Kisling*, of the poet *Muselli*, of the wife of the producer Jean Renoir, the actress, *Catherine Hessling*, of his own wife, the former *Alice Princet*, whose Madonna beauty "with great gentle eyes and beautiful hair", combined with a certain air of wildness "which harmonised strangely with her Madonna-like face",[2] must have been particularly inspiring to Derain.

But immediately afterwards Derain gave himself up to a sort of

[1] At that time Carrà had a great admiration for Derain.   [2] Gertrude Stein, *Autobiography*.

palpable voluptuousness, and it seemed as though from now on his main ambition was to convey the texture of a granulous nutshell, or the precious transparency of grapes, or the rough surface of a terracotta jug. Two or three happy tones, and off the picture goes to the Vollard of the new generation, the shrewd but straightforward Paul Guillaume, who, together with the Rosenbergs, Hessel and one or two others, administers the finances of the capital of European painting.

But Derain seems more and more to be "smothering the fervour of his early experiments and his fruitful anxieties under the indifference of a sceptic who has been defeated by knowing too many masterpieces." His nudes, his series of portraits, still reveal the intelligence and the hand of a painter. Sometimes the poetry is still present, but his work betrays a certain weariness. "His youth has flown", wrote Jacques Emil Blanche for a *cahier*, *Pour ou contre Derain*, which Raymond Cogniat compiled on my behalf. But I am inclined to agree with Pierre Courthion that in his most recent landscape painting Derain recovers something of his youthful spirit; in his trees, forests and pale springtime scenes in even greens. By some miracle, these landscapes no longer contain any traces of that liquid ground painting for which he has been often reproached.

Derain is indeed a sceptic. But I think he has been harmed not so much by knowledge of too many masterpieces as by a desire to compromise with public taste (there was also a trace of this in Renoir's work) and by wanting to lead a life of ease, for which artists in princely palaces, even if they live a cloistered existence, must be prepared to sacrifice something of their art. Not everyone has Picasso's strength of character or Matisse's good sense.

Hemingway maintains that Picasso[1] is a business man; but he has always been ashamed of being seen in a car. And as for Matisse,[2]

---

[1] "Picasso! He was always miserable at having to sell pictures. When the deal was over the loss of his pictures always made him profoundly sad, and for several days he no longer wanted to work" (from the memoirs of Fernande Olivier, who was Picasso's first companion, faithful *à la mode de Montmartre*).

[2] In this respect, too, Matisse can serve as a guide and as an example. Severini writes: "At the basis of his work (apart from the various academies he attended) is a picture by Cézanne which he bought from Vollard at the cost of great sacrifice when he was very poor and when a Cézanne was worth very little on the Paris market. Matisse has kept this picture by him for thirty-seven years. He and his courageous companion struggled as best they could through immense material hardship, but the Cézanne was never sacrificed. Matisse derived great strength from this picture: 'It has borne me up in the critical moments of my adventures as an artist. I drew my faith and my perseverance from

he has always expressed gratitude when I have told him of a cheap wine, even in the days when the best bottle of wine cost less than five or six francs.

Can we still place hope in Derain? Whatever happens, we must not forget that he will leave to posterity about fifty paintings worthy of the museums which inspired them.

As for Kess Van Dongen (born 1876), who in his youth had a taste for contrasts and who was amongst the most disquietening of the Fauves, it is enough to say that he has added to the art of female portrait painting a version of his own which all the most elegant and emancipated Parisiennes from 1920 to 1940 wished to resemble. It might be worth quoting J. E. Blanche's criticism: "His faces as naked as the bodies of the mannequins in the great fashion houses, symbols of the post-war period, will stand as formidable penal certificates."

it.' He once refused an offer of over a million francs for it from an American collector. In 1936 he gave it to the Petit Palais so that all the artists in Paris could benefit by its teaching as he had. This picture is *Les Trois Baigneuses*, of which there exist many studies and variations, all leading up to this final version."

Wooden Cannons

MATISSE declared a few years ago that Fauvism originated in a courageous return to *la pureté des moyens*. But this could obviously be said of other tendencies, and it is unsound in so far as it suggests that artists who were not lucky enough to play a part in the movement lacked this much-vaunted purity of means. Seurat's means were no less pure than those of Matisse, the Fauve. But although Fauvism, as we have seen, can be looked upon as the conclusion of nineteenth-century art in France, one should also recognise that it inaugurated, although perhaps unconsciously, a whole series of experiments which are interesting in themselves and not, as was the case with the preceding tendencies, merely on account of their aims. Impressionism, Symbolism, Divisionism and, in England, the Pre-Rephaelite movement (J. B. Millais, Holman Hunt, J. M. Strudwick and above all Rossetti, whose meticulous chromolithographs extolled the haunting memory of beauty in bygone days); the Pre-Raphaelite derivations in France (Puvis de Chavannes, of whom Cézanne said, *"C'est bien imité"*, and Gustave Moreau—according to Salvador Dali *"genre hallucinant-digestif"*); the Helvetico-Teutonic complications in Boecklin's dark and sepulchral work; the complex paintings of a Christian-socialising character (Hodler)—all these æsthetic creeds claimed, rightly or wrongly, to have helped the artist to express himself freely, to have provided him with means for painting living and modern pictures. After the Fauves, the Cubists claimed to have discovered the truth, and they did indeed inaugurate the art of our century with a really solemn statement. But, almost as though Cubism had been frightened by the truth it had discovered, it retracted and seemed to wish to be forgotten. Undoubtedly it was fear that he might impose a new discipline on art by means of Cubism which made Picasso draw back when he had already accepted the "Cubist" label. The twentieth-century artist wants freedom because never has the existence of art been so threatened by politicians as it is to-day. And

54

politicians wish to turn art into an instrument for their propaganda, not so much because they believe in the efficacy of art as because they cannot tolerate the thought of anyone managing to escape their control.

From 1905 to 1940 a hundred different tendencies started up. Sometimes artists let themselves be ensnared, but the most genuine ones refused to become entangled even in the knots of their own theories. Just as Picasso escaped from Cubism, so Severini and Carrà broke loose from the fetters of Futurism, De Chirico and Carrà freed themselves from the spell of metaphysics—despite its stupendous fascination —and Kandinsky and Klee escaped by miracle from Expressionism and Mirò from Surrealism. But they were not all equally lucky. Indeed, we must not forget the example of Renoir, who became a refugee from Impressionism. But Renoir was an exception for his time. In the twentieth century the contrary attitude, closed-minded faithfulness to a doctrine, is the exception. Like Mauriac's *pure of heart*, however, the twentieth-century Signacs—and they do exist—are men without history.

But I should be failing in my duty as an impartial chronicler if I did not point out that this supreme liberty, to which we owe work of great value, introduced one of the most intolerant periods in the history of art. This must be due to one of those fatal contradictions in human nature, or there may be another explanation which escapes my humble judgment. However it may be, while some people threaten to burn museums, others want to burn Picasso's pictures in the name of Kandinsky or Klee; others accept Picasso, but want to drag Matisse in the mud. And here I am not referring to the enemies of modern art, who aim at throwing all modern artists into the same madhouse, and have even attempted to do so. When I tried to make *XXème Siècle* into a review open to all tendencies, I was suspected of God knows what sinister motives. But now that I have revealed this personal secret I must continue my survey, or, rather, turn back.

We are now back in the first years of the century. In the preceding chapter we made the acquaintance of Matisse, Vlaminck, Derain and others. Now we must meet Picasso, Braque, Severini, La Fresnaye and their friends.

Towards 1905–6, as I have already pointed out, some influence of

Cézanne could be observed in the work of young painters, but we cannot say that his lesson was entirely understood at that time. And it was only thanks to one of the strangest deviations ever recorded in the history of art that Cézanne came to be thoroughly understood a few years later. This happened through the study of Negro idols unearthed in the junk shops of Paris by Vlaminck, and then brought to Picasso's attention by Matisse. Matisse and Picasso had met at the house of the Steins, who, ever since they had first become infatuated with modern art, went about collecting the most important pictures by these two painters. This infatuation began in Florence as a result of seeing Cézanne's first pictures while they were staying at the villa belonging to the American, Loeser, whom I mentioned at the beginning of this book.

Pablo Ruiz (Picasso is the name of his mother, who was of Genoese origin), the infant prodigy of modern painting, arrived in Paris from his native Spain towards the end of the last century when he was sixteen or seventeen years old (he was born in Malaga, 1881). His first exhibition, which Gustave Coquiot got up in Vollard's gallery in the rue Lafitte, dates from 1901, six years after Cézanne's first personal exhibition. By 1906, when Severini and Modigliani came to Paris, Picasso had already painted his famous *La Vie* and was working on the portrait of Gertrude Stein, the painting in which critics see a first serious quest for form on the lines already hinted at in a few of his earlier works—works, as it were, *hors série*.

The pictures Vollard exhibited betrayed the influence of Toulouse-Lautrec on this youth, who so far in the whole of Paris only knew Montmartre. But between 1902 and 1905 the pictures of his so-called Blue period already reveal a more personal artist; an extremely able one who sees the spectacle of daily life with the eyes of a Pre-Raphaelite and reveals its dramatic intensity with profound and frank stupefaction. Pierre Mac-Orlan has described the adolescent girls who inspired a whole series of Picasso's paintings of that time: "They used to come and go between the hospital and the slum looking more wretched than men. Prostitution was forbidden to them. One of them who was eighteen, which, I believe, is the legal age, somehow got into a brothel in the *Ecole Militaire* district. One day she came back to the slum

56

where I used to live with four or five other fellows. She looked happy. She was well dressed. She had grown fatter. . . ." Like the girl described by Pierre Mac-Orlan, Picasso's heroines, the sisters of those youths he painted in his Rose period (1905–7), which was a sort of appendix to the Blue period, could only hope for salvation in the brothel. At the age of twenty, this was Picasso's only optimism, and his work must be considered, as Christian Zervos rightly remarks, as a sort of journal "in which the artist systematically noted down the scenes which inspired his brush or his pencil".

Towards 1907 Picasso felt he needed to react against the sentimentality of harlequins, acrobats and the painful childbearing of ecstatic girls; to free himself from what the French call *le coté émouvant et littéraire de la peinture*. Compared with *La Hollandaise*, Gertrude Stein's portrait is a work of powerful structure. Obviously the problem of how to construct human forms had already begun to torment Picasso, who repudiates with this work of true plastic strength what one might call the "literary complex" in painting as well as the supposed conquests of Impressionism and Divisionism. It was then that Negro art revealed to him a new technique of construction and enabled him to give definite orientation to his researches. The "monumental" quality of Negro sculpture shows a rough but masterful instinct for construction. It was this kind of construction, arising from an instinctive need to simplify forms, that Picasso adopted during his Negro period (1908–9). And it was without doubt the study of these works of Picasso's Negro period, with their perhaps only surface relationship with Cézanne's architecture, which enabled Derain and Braque to understand Cézanne, who had died just under two years earlier (October 22, 1906) and whose famous dictum, "*Traitez la nature par le cylindre, la sphère, le cône*", was already beginning to preoccupy the more intelligent young painters. In the summer of 1910 Picasso, with *Le Moulin à huile*, Derain (who also passed through a Negro period, as we have seen), with his *Pont de Cagnes*, and Braque found themselves grouped together on the threshold of Cubism. But Cubism hadn't yet been reached. They had got no further than landscapes of an audacious Cézannesque design.

Braque's landscapes (Picasso never exhibited) were refused by the jury of the *Salon d'Automne*, despite the intervention of Matisse, who later said that Braque had sent in *cubes* (actually they were houses shaped like dice). Just as in the case of Impressionism, the name existed before the thing named. And perhaps it was this chance word which gave Picasso—always very sensitive to the slightest allusion—the idea of the cubic interpretation of nature which gave rise to Cubism.

The first historian of the group, the poet Guillaume Apollinaire, "an amazingly brilliant man who took up any subject which came his way, whether he was familiar with it or not, saw all its possibilities in a flash, leapt on it with wit and imagination and developed it further than any expert",[1] gives one to understand that Cubism was invented by Picasso and Braque together. But the beautiful Fernande Olivier, in her memoirs, *Picasso et ses Amis*, says that Braque, "with his typical Norman diffidence, only arrived at Cubism after an instinctive revulsion against it. During a discussion on Cubism at Picasso's house, Braque was unwilling to allow himself to be won over to Cubism, in spite of all Picasso's arguments, which were particularly clear on that day. . . .

" 'But', replied Braque in the end, 'despite your explanations you paint as though you were trying to make us eat tough meat or drink petrol.' What took place in his mind after this profession of faith? How did he manage to change his mind so quickly? How was it that he suddenly came to believe in the future of Cubism? I don't know. But not long afterwards, at the *Salon des Indépendants*, he exhibited a large Cubist picture which he must have painted in secret. He had mentioned it to no one, not even to its inspirer, Picasso. Perhaps he was hoping to gather the fruits of the new formula himself? It might have been worth attempting to do so, since Picasso never exhibited. Picasso, who had only just revealed his new manner to his intimate friends, felt rather indignant."

But all this is without importance, and in any case feminine evidence of this kind is always rather suspect. It is Cubism's future development, rather than Fernande Olivier's evidence, which really proves that Picasso was always the inventor and Braque the approver and

[1] Gertrude Stein, *Autobiography*.

regulator. Moreover, we know that, even without Cubism, Picasso would have been a great artist, whereas Braque would probably have remained the modest landscape painter dear to Gustave Coquiot —and Cubism made him one of the greatest artists of our time. In other words, if Picasso is the soul of Cubism, Braque *is* Cubism; he gave it Cartesian foundations and incorporated it into the French tradition.

But we still do not know what on earth Cubism is.

At the time when it was beginning, a critic wrote: "There are three principles on which Cubism is based: pure painting (I put this first as being fundamental), reality perceived in its solidity and gravity, and the integral representation of things."

Maurice Raynal, the celebrated theoretician of Cubism, defined what he meant by "pure painting"—and we must all agree—as follows: "It is painting which is neither descriptive, nor anecdotal, nor psychological, nor moral, nor sentimental, nor pedagogical, nor, lastly, decorative. . . . In short, painting must only be an art deriving from the study of forms for a disinterested end. . . ." This means, as a critic explained, that sentiment, expression, poetic magic and so forth must result from the harmony of the pictorial elements alone—lines, tones, values, volumes and chiaroscuro—and from their intrinsic quality; just as in music, where sentiment, expression, poetic magic and so on result from the combination and intimate quality of the notes and their harmony—and not from the subject indicated for the benefit of the audience in the title or programme.

The second principle—namely, "reality interpreted in its solidity and gravity"—is the side of Cubism directly in contrast with the rigid interpretation of Impressionist theory. Impressionism conceived the visible world as an aggregate of light vibrations, a flowing stream in which forms are only differentiated by a greater or lesser intensity of tone and their varying distribution (agglomerative sympathy and the contrast of prismatic colours). Cubism set out to re-establish the tangible solidity, the static structure, the permanent materiality (perceived through the combination of the organ of sight with the other senses) over and above the accidents of lighting and colour. Impressionism rejected outline and contour. Cubism proclaimed the existence of line and studied the measurements of the planes it circumscribed.

59

As for the third and last principle, the integral representation of things, we can say that it consists in representing the object not in its visual aspect, but in its material and immaterial structure, in its complete materiality and spirituality.

Cubism therefore repudiated the representation of the object as it is reflected on the retina of the eye, but obviously it did create an art entirely abstracted from the object. Cubist paintings remain landscapes, still-lifes and portraits. In this sense, Picasso, perhaps involuntarily, went beyond Cubism, and so did Mondrian and the Neo-Plastics, Dada and the abstract painters.

For the present, however, we are only dealing with the origins of the movement.

The Impressionists' research work was based on physics, but the Cubists needed a mathematician. This mathematician presented himself in the shape of Princet, who became Alice Derain's first husband after he had lived with her for many years. From what might be called the *domestic* point of view, Cubism cost Princet the dearest love of his life; it caused the final break between Picasso and 'la belle Fernande', who felt that she was being neglected and could not, like Paolo di Dono's wife, content herself with the mere spiritual enjoyment of her companion. Finally, Cubism stole the delicious Eva from Marcoussis and gave her in atonement to Picasso. It would be ridiculous to speak of these things had they not influenced the destiny of Cubism. The *Ma jolie* with which Picasso "stabbed to death a wonderful Cubist picture",[1] and with it the whole of Cubism, which, according to Braque, should have refused to imitate what should really be created,[2] was merely, as Gertrude Stein tells us, Picasso's gentle request to Eva on the eve of their elopement. But let us return to Cubism.

Between 1911 and 1913 Picasso and Braque seemed determined to strive after the absolute, and even renounced the fascination of colour. An almost uniform grey was the only colour used by the Cubists during the early years. "*Chères grisailles*", as André Breton called them, "*où tout finit et recommence, pareilles à ces toits que le peintre voit de sa fenêtre, inclinés sous la grande voile du ciel de Paris, aux nuages changeantes. La même*

[1] C. Belli, *K.N.*
[2] Guillaume Apollinaire: "Man needed to make inanimate objects walk. Knowing no other means of locomotion than his legs, he invented the wheel."

fumée légère selon l'heure à peine un peu plus claire, un peu plus sombre que le ciel, évoque seul la vie humaine par étages et par cases. . . ."

Among the other Cubists who exhibited with Braque at the *Salon des Indépendants* of 1910 were Jean Metzinger, Robert Delaunay, Le Fauconnier, and Marie Laurencin, *"qui frôle le cubisme de ses ailes"* —the muse of the poet Apollinaire. Apollinaire's portrait was exhibited by Jean Metzinger; it was appropriate that the first Cubist portrait should have been that of the first historian of the movement. The following year the Cubists got a whole room to themselves. The artists I have already mentioned were joined by Albert Gleizes and Fernand Léger. Delaunay (who had, with an eye to business, ferreted out and managed to gain possession of the most striking Douanier Rousseaus) exhibited *La Tour*, the famous Eiffel Tower, which looks, with all its planes and sections, as though it had been built on purpose to serve as a model for the Cubists. Fernand Léger translated into Cubist language a *Nu dans un Paysage*.

The first exhibition the Cubists held outside France took place in Brussels, and in the catalogue of this exhibition Guillaume Apollinaire for the first time accepted the terms "Cubism" and "Cubists" on behalf of the exhibitors.

The Cubist exhibition at the *Salon d'Automne* towards the end of 1911 aroused an outburst of jeers in the Press similar to those provoked by the first Impressionist exhibitions. Nevertheless, the three Duchamp brothers, Marcel, the sculptor Duchamp-Villon and the engraver Jacques Villon, who has only won distinction in recent years, continued to adhere to Cubism. New collective manifestations took place in 1911 at the *Galerie d'Art Contemporain* and in 1912 at the *Salon des Indépendants*, at which a newcomer, Juan Gris, also appeared. Juan Gris had found a master and a providential host in Picasso: a lesson, a hot dish, and a little place squeezed in for him on the only table cloth. In May, 1912, Barcelona welcomed the young French painters with enthusiasm (this is a fabrication of Apollinaire's). In June of the same year they got up an exhibition at Rouen, and it was here that Picabia produced his first Cubist pictures.

Pierre Courthion calls this the Doric period of Cubism. For Picasso and Braque it was above all *"un moyen d'approfondir, de sonder de nouvelles et mystérieuses profondeurs*", whereas for all the others, including Juan Gris and Léger, at least in their early works, it was only a technique or a formula. Braque, who arrived at Cubism direct from Cézanne, and never passed through equatorial Africa, produced calmer and less dramatic work than Picasso, who here and there seemed to echo the brutality of black Spain.

Between the Doric period and what I shall call the Ionic period of Cubism comes Italian Futurism. Futurism had already published its famous manifesto, "We have kept watch all night", in *Le Figaro* on February 20, 1909. At this point I must pay tribute to Severini's prudence: by advising Boccioni, Carrà and Russolo to pay a short but salutary visit to Paris, Severini's foresight and love of his native country managed to prevent the epithet "Italian" from once again becoming synonymous with "burlesque". Even Corrado Pavolini, who is no eagle, recognised that Futurism was nothing but "the insertion of a dynamic element into the rigid Cubist mathematics, as one sees if one makes a study of the respective chronological developments in the two schools". Whoever troubles to read the Futurist manifestoes will see that the well-known Futurist dynamism was originally a return to Impressionism, with the added intention of outdoing it in speed. Balla, who had unveiled Impressionism to Severini and Boccioni in 1903–4, found no better way of expressing the dynamism of a little dog in paint than to depict it with eight or more legs. The Impressionists tried to perpetuate the vibrations of light by fixing them with the colours of the prism. The Futurists declared that the artist should interest himself instead in the vibrations of motors, whether human or mechanical. Corrado Pavolini, in *Cubism, Futurism and Expressionism*, maintained that the two outstanding figures in the group were Umberto Boccioni and Carrà, and he refused to consider Severini—he judged him over-hastily as a decorator.

I do not wish to deny the great qualities of Carrà[1] who, like Soffici (at first hostile to Cubism, but later converted by Valentine de Saint Point's *Manifeste futuriste de la Luxure*), learnt how to weave his powerful webs of colour from the Cubists.

---

[1] Apollinaire used to speak of Rouault à propos of Carrà. Carrà is certainly and incontestably a genuine painter, but he has nothing in common with Rouault.

But the importance of Severini is of a totally different kind. "Gino Severini", wrote Raymond Escholier in *La Peinture du XXème Siècle*, "the prince of Futurism, owes something to Cubism, if I may say so; but Cubism is equally indebted to him. It was thanks to Severini, who has lived in Paris since 1906 and who in 1912 painted *La Danse du Pan Pan à Monico* and in 1913 *L'Autobus*, that the Cubists abandoned their doleful chiaroscuro and returned almost immediately afterwards to the light and joyful colours and the vivid tones La Fresnaye used in painting *L'Artillerie*. *La Danse du Pan Pan* had been exhibited at the Futurist exhibition in Paris in February, 1912, and it constituted their first concrete achievement. Boccioni, Carrà, Russolo and Severini met in Paris for the occasion. On the whole, the critics received this exhibition with a certain sympathy, but no one failed to notice that Boccioni, "the conscience of Futurism", had derived his "means" from Picasso. All the works exhibited revealed the Impressionist and Neo-Impressionist origins of the new movement, though the idea of returning frankly to the "subject" was incontestably Futurist.

"To Futurism Severini brought the pure colours of the artist to whom he owed a part of his formation—Seurat—for he alone understood Seurat's poetic intentions. In an essay on Severini, Germain Bazin admits that at a certain moment in French painting Severini's work was more 'actual' than the work of Picasso himself. *La Danse du Pan Pan* is unquestionably the masterpiece of Futurism. In it one distinctly feels the gulf separating Cubism from Futurism. Cubism aimed at being a coercive force, Futurism was a liberating force. Picasso pursued form to its very end and reduced it to its final lineaments or submitted it to an automatic rhythm, but Severini set form free.[1] This dance, with its furious rhythm, seems to represent the multiplicity of sensations caused by intoxication—which produces a sense of the ubiquity of forms endlessly rotating and replacing each other. This desperate attempt to introduce into space a sensation of the duration of time reveals the cinematographic tendency in painting. But it was only twenty years later that the cinema achieved the possibilities already perceived by Severini."

[1] This Boccioni later achieved in sculpture, and he can be considered the first modern sculptor of our age. The Rumanian Brancusi is certainly a masterly inventor of plastic form, but I hesitate to call him a sculptor.

Through Severini's merit (or fault), Cubism ceased to be a closed art and, in the words of Ozenfant and Jeanneret, it abandoned its *"limitation austère, ascétique des moyens"*. But Severini was not the only one to shoulder this great responsibility. We have seen how Picasso introduced a melodramatic *Ma jolie* into the melody of one of his paintings. Little by little the Cubist structure of his paintings, like Braque's, became a scaffolding behind which one perceives the body and pegs of violins, guitar roses, a bull-fighter's moustache or the velvet eyes of some disquietening female prisoner. And then Picasso took to glueing things on to his canvas. One day it would be Gertrude Stein's visiting card, another day a piece of newspaper (this habit was immediately imitated by Braque, unless it was Braque who first thought of introducing a realistic element into the unreal life of a picture), and, finally, he glued on a clay pipe. This was the period during which Cubist pictures tried to become objects, or, as Maurice Raynal said, a species of totems. But straightway they developed into bull-fighters' moustaches and the velvety eyes of female prisoners. Letters, first introduced as shapes, began to form themselves into words and to tell a story. Thus ended the Doric period of Cubism. The works belonging to the years 1913–14 had ceased to be *"à la peinture, telle qu'on l'avait envisagée jusqu'ici, ce que la musique est à la littérature"*, as Apollinaire had prophesied. Although Picasso had declared that as painting has its own beauty, beauty could be made abstract on condition that it remained pictorial, he excused himself many years later and affirmed that man has an instinctive need to discover some sort of resemblance in an abstract work: "trace anywhere within a circle two horizontal lines and one vertical line, and everyone will see it as a face." But Braque said the opposite: "One cannot arrive at an abstraction if one starts out from an abstraction. It would be as though the work had never taken place. To arrive at an abstraction one must start out from nature, and to start out from nature means finding a subject. If one loses touch with nature one inevitably ends up with *decoration*." Therefore the Futurists were right. In the end even Apollinaire realised this and began to collect together all the *avantgarde* tendencies around Futurism. But Marinetti, doubtless through fear of being eclipsed by the poet whom Douanier Rousseau had already crowned with laurels, avoided the danger by restricting Futurism to "the limits and character of an Italian movement". Apollinaire's modest contribution to Futurism was a rather silly manifesto entitled *L'Anti-tradition Futuriste* (June 29, 1913), which handed out bouquets to Picasso and Giannattasio, to himself and to Manzella-Frontini. And that was his only contribution. Then, disillusioned, Apollinaire founded *L'Orphisme* with Robert Delaunay, who all unknowingly was the most Futurist of the Cubist painters. "I like movement to break through lines. A motor car is a downright modern creation, a fact." So wrote Delaunay and used his theory of simultaneous contrasts to try to build up "a technique we need to extend to many other activities—for instance, coloured films. The art of movement ought to bear the imprint of our epoch".

The renunciation of ascetism in painting made endless critics weep unlimited tears. Now, at a distance of so many years, those passionate demonstrations of sorrow which accompanied the conclusion of the first Cubist movement seem, as in fact they were, rather hypocritical. The sorrowing critics no doubt wanted to be able to list the Cubists and then forget them. How are we to believe that people who were at best only capable of enjoying an operetta were sincerely convinced by the abstract beauty of pure painting, when it aroused such painful perplexity in Picasso and Braque themselves? These critics still persist in calumniating the second Cubist movement, and describe it as a kind of abstract Academicism. But in my opinion it is one of the most fruitful periods of French painting. Although Braque (born at Argenteuil, 1881) never lost sight of Picasso, he embarked on a series of experiments which later reached perfection in work after work. He was perpetually torn between wanting to make "a direct transcription of appearances" and an ever-growing need for invention. Juan Gris began to find out, as he himself put it, if not what to do, at least what *not* to do. Severini and Roger de la Fresnaye (born at Le Mans, 1885, died at Grasse, 1925) reacted against the general trend which now, after the discipline of the heroic period, allowed the widest freedom of technique and subject, and they went in search of a system. The first Cubist sculptors, Lipchitz and Laurens, appeared on the horizon. Zadkine and Modigliani allowed themselves to be tempted by the movement. Picasso, *"qui conduit le bal"*, taught people how to interpret the object, and although he ended by accepting "the magical and dangerous forces lying dormant in metal", he prevented Cubist colours from becoming imitations of the colours represented. The logical distortion of the object, which originated with Cézanne, is in Picasso's work—just as it was later to become in Braque's, who goes over all Picasso's inventions and carries them to their supreme expression— a complete plastic *ars poetica* of distortion. The torment of invention concentrated even upon colour itself. Braque had learnt all the secrets of the distempering business from his father, who was the proprietor of a little working painter's business, and so he was able to teach the Cubists to mix sand and plaster with their paints and to imitate marble and wood. And then the outbreak of the war put an end to Braque's experiments. Léger,[1] who was also mobilised, was put on to designing cannon breeches (when towards 1918 he was able to take up painting again, this experience gave him the idea of constructing his pictures as though they were complicated machines), but Braque was sent off to the front. There he obtained two *citations*, but three years later he was horribly wounded, operated on and discharged. Picasso, Severini and Gris remained in Paris. One night, writes Gertrude Stein, they saw a large wooden cannon being drawn along the Boulevard Raspail. "We are the fellows who invented that", said Picasso. Such a statement would have been enough to make a German philosopher blame the Cubists for the Kaiser's war. But what Picasso meant was that, just as soldiers replaced bronze cannons with wooden ones, so the Cubists painted false bottles and glasses. For just as the wooden cannons were not meant to be fired off, but were only supposed to represent cannons, so it would have been useless and foolish to paint real bottles and glasses to look as though one could gulp down a glass of something. The Cubists had no desire to make their spectators thirsty.

[1] "I am satisfied", declared Léger in 1918, "if in a flat a picture of mine dominates the room in which it is hanging, if it imposes itself upon everything, people and furniture. It must be the most important personage. I detest modest painting. I take my subjects from all over the place. I love the forms which modern industry has created, and I use them—those steels with a thousand coloured reflections both more delicate and stronger than the so-called classical subjects. I maintain that a machine gun or the breech of a 75-mm. cannon are more worth-while painting than four apples on a table or a landscape at St. Cloud, and this without going in for Futurism." However, when it is a matter of using machine guns and 75-mm. guns, even in a war like the recent one, Léger finds that it is wiser to let others get on with it, and to get as far away as possible himself.

Gleizes and Metzinger, who have a really innate leaning towards Academicism, were the theoreticians of the new Cubism, and it obviously had very little in common with the first kind. Most of the French painters were at the Front, and so was the poet Guillaume Apollinaire (he died from his wounds on the night of the Armistice while the crowd was shouting "*A bas Guillaume*" under his windows). Marcel Duchamp and Picabia crossed the Atlantic to the United States, and there they went on introducing realities and certainties (pieces of glass, scraps of newspaper, bits of metal, bicycle wheels, etc.) into the world of illusion. In Switzerland the Alsatian Arp, who felt ill at ease in France on account of his origin, got together with Eggeling, Jango, Augusto Giacometti and the poets Ball and Tzara, and founded a movement which later joined up with Marcel Duchamp and Picabia's movement and became Dadaism. Later on we shall examine the consequences of Cubism, for every artist of intelligence owes something to it.

Severini felt that Picasso's extreme individualism ought to be counterbalanced by a sort of impersonal art; that is to say, art based on fixed rules and free from the tyranny of personality, and La Fresnaye, Léger, Metzinger and Gleizes had become preoccupied in a similar way and, towards 1920, they formed a group known as the *Section d'Or*. Severini was the first to abandon the systematic distortion of the object and to give it back its more usual shape, its so-called "standard" shape, as it was later developed by the Purists. It was not that he allowed himself to be too obsessed with the fate of the object. He was really interested in the relationship between objects, the plastic and mathematical relationships. He seemed to want to fulfil Plato's ideal, and make mathematics the basis of culture; and he collected his studies into a book on the æsthetics of numbers six years before Matila C. Ghyka's more famous work on the same subject.

Severini had only just accepted Cubism and was already thinking of incorporating it into Classicism when a scandal broke out. Picasso suddenly deserted Cubism and began to paint portraits and figures in the manner of Ingres (*Portrait de Mme. Picasso*, 1917). His devotees proclaimed in vain that these portraits were also creations of the spirit and exactly like his Cubist work. The Cubists were perplexed, and critics like Coquiot, who had admired Picasso's Blue and Rose periods and could not forgive him for his *"immondices fétides"*, now burst into mad laughter. Actually, the first paintings of Picasso's Ingres period seem to me no more than a mere pause, a necessary point of reference before passing from the free interpretation of the object to its geometrical transfiguration. For Picasso, even more openly than the other painters, has geometry in mind. And did not Ingres say: *"Les belles formes sont des plans droits avec des rondeurs"*? And could Picasso, between Cubism and his recent incursions into the core of "abstract" orthodoxy, have found a more precise point of reference than this?

Between 1917 and 1921 Picasso's geometrical paintings alternated with those in the Ingres style, and they are interesting in an entirely different way. *Les Musiciens* and *Mardi Gras* in the Paul Rosenberg Collection are obviously light and pleasing, but they have a spirituality, in their geometrical lightness, which we look for in vain in the *Portrait de Mme. Picasso* of 1917 and *l'Arlequin* of the same year.

But when Picasso's "sentiment" had become sufficiently imbued with crystalline geometry (this happened towards 1922), the Harlequins in the manner of Ingres turned into transparent Picassoesque creations, and even M. Ingres himself would have taken off his hat to them. It is even tempting to think that the only thing Ingres lacked in order to surpass himself was the experience of the artists who reached maturity between 1911 and 1920.

When we compare this Picasso with the Cubist one of the previous period, we see how the later work involves more immediate transcriptions of form and is closer to nature than the former. This may seem paradoxical, but Picasso has been able to prove that what we call Classicism is even further removed from the real appearance of the object than the Cubist interpretation. And Severini, who in the meantime had painted the wonderful frescoes at Montegufoni, one of his most important achievements, now arrived at the very same conclusion along another route. Severini discovered that the great masters of the fifteenth century managed to avoid the temptations of abstraction not by drawing closer to nature, but by moving further away.

In his "Classical" work, Picasso—who had visited Italy in the meantime—no sooner accentuated the volumes, or made them undergo an abstract distortion (thereby creating the famous monumental series), than the figures, although freed in a fuller, more Raphael-like rhythm, began to assume an almost naturalistic expression; "they no longer think of anything", as Renoir would have said.

All this had already become the subject of aphorism, but no one had yet attempted to demonstrate it in painting.

The result of the demonstration was that all the followers of Cubism immediately deserted it *en masse*. They were terrified of suddenly discovering that they had fallen into a new naturalism; and this is what inevitably did happen to the most sincere amongst them, to Severini,[1] La Fresnaye and others. Picasso and Braque managed to escape this danger, the former by a sudden "return to Greece", the latter by clinging desperately to the object.

But materialistic critics interpreted this mass desertion as a consequence of the disastrous auction sale, in 1921, of the collection of the German Kahnweiler, the Cubists' first dealer, who but for the war would have become—according to *la belle Fernande*—"the biggest dealer in Paris, and extremely rich". But after what had happened to the Impressionists (in 1875 twenty pictures by Renoir, Claude Monet, Sisley and Berthe Morisot had been sold in the Hôtel Drouot for 2,150 francs, and at another sale in 1877 sixteen pictures by Renoir were valued at 2,005 francs), the Cubists need not have expected desperate consequences as a result of the Kahnweiler fiasco. (Braque tried in vain to defend Kahnweiler by attacking the official valuer, the merchant Hessel.) In fact, the Cubists could easily have foreseen what actually did happen, and they had plenty of grounds for hope. To-day the works of the masters of Cubism are highly prized by collectors.

---

[1] Herbin and Metzinger at once attempted to fall in line with Severini, but an artist cannot adopt a ready-made language; he must find it for himself; and Herbin and Metzinger did not allow themselves time. On this subject, Severini said to me: "The fear the Cubists had of suddenly finding themselves faced with a kind of naturalism was justifiable and, indeed, a few of them, the weak ones, succumbed. But where La Fresnaye and myself are concerned, it was not so much naturalism that we hit up against as a transcendental realism of classical tendency.

"I personally began to like the game, especially since there grew up in Paris such a cult for the abstract, the bizarre and the *trouvaille* at all costs. It was more dignified and more moral, I thought, to explore the new road to the end, while inwardly remaining free to choose another at any moment."

As Maurice Raynal wrote: "Had La Fresnaye, who died so prematurely, really the capability of achieving work as lyrical and human as that of Corot or Ingres? Or were his latest achievements the expression of a spiritually sensitive delicately adorned rather 'Pléiade' temperament—a temperament formed to express only the less marked aspects of human reality? I myself rather incline to the latter opinion."

F

One man, with an indomitable will worthy of the Inquisition, managed to save Cubism at the hour of danger. This was Juan Gris (born, Madrid, 1887; died, Paris, 1927). Fernande Olivier, who loathed Cubism as being responsible for her youthful errors, says that Juan Gris, "without great talent, but shrewd, soon followed the movement. He studied what we could call the 'mechanics of Cubism' and used it with some sort of intelligence, but with no art, and he never got beyond it. He was able to create a solid position for himself and keep it. Cubism was extremely useful to many artists who would not have known how to get on without it".

I got to know Gris in Montparnasse in 1924. At that time he was the despot of the "mechanics of Cubism" (if there is such a thing!), and he was enclosing his favourite objects, guitars, squares, coffee-pots and fruit-baskets in sombre geometrical ideograms.[1] Whenever he chanced to express his ideas, he always said the exact opposite of anything he heard anyone else say. For example, were Braque to say, "I love measure which corrects emotion", Gris would announce in his strong Spanish accent: "I love emotion which corrects measure." (And there was less and less trace of emotion in his pictures.) He was bent on "humanising" painting, and he would say: "Cézanne made a cylinder out of a bottle and I make a bottle out of a cylinder. Cézanne went towards architecture, I start out and move away from architecture." But when I allowed myself to call the second period of Cubism "Ionic", I wasn't thinking of Juan Gris and "his extremely delicate sense of values" at all. In fact, if any artist of the second Cubism was endeavouring to go back to the severity of the Doric period, it was surely Juan Gris, the inquisitor.

Marcoussis (born, Warsaw, 1883; died, Dax, 1939) was another "Ionic" painter who brought Oriental elegance and delicacy to Cubism. And, anyway, if we judge by results, the style of a newcomer,

[1] Severe geometrical rules, not intuitive ones like Picasso's, were discovered by Gris and Severini between 1916 and 1925. The sculptor Lipchitz also took part in these researches into geometrical relations (the rotations of forms round an axis, etc.). In the Montegufoni frescoes, in the pictures in the Van der Meulen Collection in Utrecht (*The Two Pulcinellas*) and Clay Bartlett Collection in Chicago (*The Card Players*), and in many other pictures of the same period, Severini had successfully applied these rules to solving the problem of how to represent human figures. Gris, on the other hand, although extremely successful as long as he was experimenting with the object, that "little sea pig" which Matisse had given the Cubists, was not equally successful with human figures.

Gris introduced Severini to Léonce Rosenberg in 1918, against the advice of Marcoussis, who at that time did not want to have a Futurist in the group.

Ozenfant, must be called Ionic too. Ozenfant, with the painter-architect Jeanneret-Le Corbusier, was the founder of Purism after 1920.

Purism codified the rights Cubism had conceded to artists, and it set out to purify the language of painting by eliminating from art all excessive sensibility, affectation, emotion and sensuality. Furthermore, it restricted the range of objects worthy of the Purist artist's attention to the commonest and most ordinary ones—those easily recognisable. There was to be no excessive sacrificing of the object's shape to the plastic building up of the painting, and the most permissible was a "marriage" of objects which could then have a common outline. As for colour, the Purists accepted the researches of the Divisionists.

If these fine theories did not enable Ozenfant and Le Corbusier (who was to reveal himself instead as the greatest architect of our time, and perhaps of the whole century) to create truly "universal" works of art, as they had hoped, they did enable Léger to simplify his over-complicated mechanical universe and forced him to turn his attention to the object. It must be admitted that the relation between colour and form is perfect in Léger. I mean his form corresponds with his colour. Other painters who are unquestionably more important than Léger have never reached such an exact equilibrium. For instance Matisse and Picasso. Matisse is too preoccupied by colour and Picasso is more inclined towards the invention of form than of colour.

Finally, André Lhote, the last theoretician of Cubism, also put forward a view of his own for finally conciliating Cubism with Classicism. Lhote, whom Raymond Escholier calls a "vehement" colourist, built up his compositions in a traditional way, but then slightly geometrised the object and allowed himself to make ludicrous substitutions of planes—recalling what happens when children reconstruct scenes with toy bricks and leave one brick out of place. These stylistic exercises, however, did not prevent him from running the art criticism of *La Nouvelle Revue Française* with great seriousness, nor from shooting an arrow at Picasso whenever the opportunity arose.

Picasso is very far from Cubism to-day, as much from the first as from the second and the third (1925), and perhaps even from the fourth (1929) period. Yet the fact is that Picasso has never really abandoned Cubism, or at least what Cubism left behind. In *Picasso*

Scultore, Enrico Prampolini, in his curious *policramatici*—he was the last and the only Futurist seriously to study the "object"—rightly observes that "Picasso's inspiration is plastic rather than pictorial, especially in the works marking the transition between his successive representative periods and epochs", and he sets out to prove that the genesis of Picasso's sculpture can be traced "in the evolution and involution of his painting". But if we want to understand the appearance of certain hallucinating forms in Picasso's painting (intermittently after 1927, but later, after 1933, almost regularly), we must look for their origin in his sculpture.

We have seen how at a given moment in his evolution Picasso was obliged to camouflage his return to naturalism by a sudden discovery of Greece; and this sometimes even reminds one of De Chirico, the Italian painter who towards 1929 managed to outdistance him in the admiration of the cosmopolitan audiences of the Russian Ballet and in that of Cocteau's beloved young men, who had been Picasso's most faithful and passionate fans for so many years. To understand how Picasso passed from his diaphonous *Métamorphoses* (which are often more hallucinating than diaphanous) to the expressionism of *Guernica* (he distributed hundreds of reproductions of *Guernica* among soldiers who went to see him during the first months of the German occupation, and for this reason, though probably not for this reason alone, journalists were forbidden to mention his name), we must remember that Picasso's painting, after 1933 (with the exception of his "Matisse" period of 1938, which I have already mentioned), is above all the work of a great sculptor.

Indeed, to anyone who knows what contortions the sculptor imposes on a Hellenic statue—to the point of the crudest metamorphosis into an Expressionist form which would delight German theoreticians—*Guernica*, which is a cry of anguish and horror provoked by the first "epic" of German aviation, and other recent works of Picasso, cannot fail to appear extremely translucent.

These largely monumental forms, which evolved from some of his youthful experiments—for example, the ones which are attempts to fuse full and side face into a single expression—originated from Picasso's obligation to accept emotions coming from everywhere, "from the sky, the earth, a piece of paper, a passer-by or from a spider web", not to mention sensations. "A person", said Picasso, "an object, a circle are *figures* which impinge on us with greater or lesser intensity. Some of them, those closest to our sensibility, work upon our affective faculties; others work upon our intellect. We must accept them all equally. My spirit requires emotions as much as it requires sensations." And one must remember that Picasso's "discoveries" during the last fifteen years are also a result of the contact between the greatest artist of our time and works of art of the remotest ages. Only someone who has deep and wide knowledge of the many works left to record man's passage on the earth can understand the meaning of Picasso's recent experiments, which *"remettent sans cesse sur la balance l'histoire de l'art"*, as Zervos so happily expressed it. A man of average culture cannot go beyond the Negro and Ingres periods. When judging the other periods, he should assume a modest attitude, as though he were contemplating, not the works of a contemporary painter, but some idol of the Cyclades, for example, or some decorated pot of the Han epoch. So-called primitive art may be spiritually closer to a modern artist's anxiety than the sweet harmonies of M. Ingres.[1] But although I agree with Matisse when he says that an artist is not the master of his own production, since "the arts have a development which does not derive from the individual alone, but from the whole accumulated energy, from the whole civilisation which precedes our own", I cannot think of Picasso without nostalgia—the inventor of Cubism, the greatest creator of plastic images that has ever lived, and an artist who has certainly not yet said his last word. Nothing can ever diminish my faith in Picasso, nor my affection for him—both as an artist who has afforded me the widest range of emotions, and as a man with whom I shared, for four long years, the cell Destiny had appointed for us in this European continent of genius at a time when no one was able or willing to save it from becoming a savage and terrifying prison.

[1] "There is an external resemblance between artistic forms", wrote Kandinsky in 1912, "which is determined by reason of great necessity. The similarity of the *inward* tendencies in a whole moral and spiritual atmosphere, the effort directed towards aims which, though they have already been pursued, have been forgotten again—in other words, this similarity in the inward trend of a whole epoch may lead logically to the adoption of forms which in earlier times successfully served to express the same tendencies. It was partly for this reason that our understanding, sympathy and affinity with the Primitives arose. In my opinion, these purist artists tried to put into their works only what had inward substance, and thus they automatically renounced every kind of external accident."

The Metaphysical Warning

WITH Futurism—and this was its chief merit—Italian art, or rather, a group of Italian artists, adopted a plastic language, universal at least in its time.

Among the first and most remarkable reactions against Futurism was that of Giorgio De Chirico. Giorgio De Chirico was born in Greece on July 10, 1888, at Volo, the ancient Pagasus or Iolcos from which the Argonauts set out to bring back the Golden Fleece. His first biographer, who was named Angelo Bardi—I know nothing about him apart from his name—tells us that on the day De Chirico was born the heat was so intense that the candles, even the unlighted ones, were melting in their sockets.

When he was seven years old, the little boy Giorgio signed his first picture, a galloping horse, and for many years it remained the most beautiful ornament in the drawing-room of the Austro-Hungarian Consul at Volo. I like to imagine that even in those days De Chirico's signature resembled his present one, that it was clear and firm like English handwriting, and as characteristic as the signature Douanier Rousseau used to trace with infinite care in closed Gothic characters.

But this precocious child was not yet considered ripe for art, and he had to learn to read and write like any other boy. It was only at the age of sixteen, when his father died, that he was able to leave the Polytechnic at Athens, where he had been entered for classes. The following year—that is to say, in 1906—young De Chirico, who had not yet heard of Cézanne, set out for Munich. It is worth observing that in those days he belonged to the world which distrusted the prestige of Paris. De Chirico's brother, Alberto Savinio, has explained the reason for this suspicion.[1] During the early years of this century, young intellectuals were attracted by Wagner and Nietzsche and thirsted for romanticism. They blamed the French for "washing their hands of all spiritual preoccupations". They thought the torch of

[1] In an essay published in *Valori Plastici*.

civilisation glowed brightest in Munich. German philosophy, music and romantic painting fired the imagination of cultured and refined adolescents and populated their first sleepless nights with bold Wagnerian images. In short, it was a generation very different from ours, which now only admires Wagner as a writer and in Nietzsche mainly singles out those indeed very illuminating pages which he devoted to his fellow countrymen.

I hasten to make these things clear because they explain De Chirico's repulsion for the naturalist æsthetics of Futurism from which the French were able to profit. During the two years he spent at the Munich Royal Academy, De Chirico was taught to reason through study of Schopenhauer and other German philosophers, but fortunately he did not learn how to paint. The gods who had already presided over his birth saw to it that De Chirico should be taught in Munich by a painter who never held a brush in his hand. If things had gone otherwise, if De Chirico had become one of those painters dear to academy teachers, and above all Bavarian ones, we should never have heard of him. Cézanne, who once aspired to the laurels of the *Salon Bouguereau*, might have had a similar fate, had he had the gift of concealing the tricks of the trade under delicate films of varnish which—as he learnt after 1880—make a painting *"inartistique et commune"*.

In 1909, when De Chirico finally came to Italy—first to Milan and then to Florence, where he spent several months—he only knew how to do a few brush strokes in the manner of Boecklin. De Chirico once said that a metaphysical picture is the work of an artist who has lost his memory: the commonest object then acquires a mystery which is impressive because of its metaphysical force. The first memory De Chirico lost was that of Boecklin's painting, and this did not come back to him again until after 1919. If painting once again became cerebral with De Chirico, this was obviously due to his personal inclination as nourished by Nietzsche and Schopenhauer. But when we consider the means he had at his disposal, we cannot fail to be amazed at his success in building up so much opulent work out of such poverty. When we look at the *Enigma on an Autumn Afternoon*, for example, we are forced to talk of a miracle, some divine or diabolical intervention—just as nothing but a miracle can account for the magic of *La Bohemienne Endormie*, by the Douanier Rousseau, who amiably said to Picasso: "We are the two greatest painters of this century. You in the *Egyptian* manner, I in the modern manner."

Obviously, Rousseau's (1844–1910) tropical mystery has nothing in common with the mystery of De Chirico, who was *quotidien* before becoming *laique*. But I am not sorry I mentioned the Douanier's name in connection with De Chirico. Fernande Olivier, who knew him, thought Le Douanier was not even intelligent, and I agree. Therefore he was the very opposite of De Chirico. But the retired Customs official, who knew nothing about the history of art and who was never taught to paint, was for all that a messenger of the gods. During the deluge caused by the advent of the new art, they ordered him to rescue the most godlike aim of painting up to the time of Manet: magic. And this magic De Chirico also recaptured in his *Enigma on an Autumn Afternoon*, painted in 1910, the very year Rousseau died— shortly after exhibiting his last picture, *Le Rêve*, at the *Salon des Indépendants*. In 1911 Rousseau's first biographer, the æsthete Wilhelm Uhde, wrote of *Le Rêve*: "Rousseau did not set out from the viewpoint of a colourist demanding that the red of the divan should produce a contrasting effect with the green of the forest. He was guided by a feeling far more majestic and much vaster in conception—namely, the emotion experienced in the presence of a strange and mysterious world. The old and uneducated Frenchman's sense of the mystery and strangeness of the world sprang from his love of nature. The erudite young Italian was inspired only by the work of man. The ingenuous 'Sunday painting' of the greatest of the *Peintres du Dimanche*, Rousseau, whom both Picasso and Apollinaire loved so dearly, is full of the Sunday feeling, for Sunday is nature's day, the one day of the week free from the boring activity of mankind. Everything about Rousseau is Sunday-like, his spirit, the mystery emanating from his virgin forests (which seem, as Uhde so well put it, to grow under our eyes '*des racines à la cîme*'), and from the dream of the beautiful Jadwiga, who, as Rousseau himself described her in verse—

> "*S'étant endormie doucement*
> *Entendait les sons d'une musette*
> *Dont jouait un charmeur bien pensant.*"

In short, the whole atmosphere is a festive Sunday, an ingenuous and gorgeous spectacle. This primitive painting (primitive because of the incipient civilisation revealed by Rousseau's dreams) is counterbalanced on the opposite side of the creative world by the art of De Chirico which carries "the overwhelming burden of so many civilisations" and endeavours to express, not the fleeting mystery of a hand laid for an instant on the heart, but the day-to-day mystery of things, the ghostlike spell of eternity. In De Chirico's painting, Rousseau's virgin forests become the forests of man, "the crazy labyrinths of perspective". The snakelike ecstasy of the beautiful Jadwiga —who in Rousseau's luxuriant earthly paradise lies on the red divan of the high officials of the Third Republic, an ultimate Eve awaiting her belated Adam—has its counterpart in the metaphysical ecstasy of *La Malinconia* in De Chirico's early work. De Chirico's Melancholy, reclining on her marble mattress, awaits no one; she does not listen to the distant sounds of a bag-pipe, but hears only the sacred silence of eternity.

I shall end this purely fortuitous comparison between the mysterious naturalism of the Frenchman and the metaphysical awe of the Italian with one last observation: both Rousseau and the early De Chirico, their different plastic intentions apart, bore the completed picture in mind. In other words, they did not aim at creating *"l'art vivant"* like their contemporaries, but only wanted to paint pictures.

De Chirico's first paintings, from the classical *Malinconia* to the romantic *Return of the Prodigal Son*, must be considered as pictures and not as painted surfaces. To discuss their plastic qualities, as some people do, is as ridiculous as to admire the precious texture of a painting which gives no emotion. The pictures of this period must be accepted or rejected, they cannot be discussed. If we accept them (and how can we refuse to accept them, if only because of the part they have played in the orientation of our minds?), we must recognise that they were painted as they should have been painted. The gods watched over their execution. In these pictures the balance between poetic inspiration and plastic execution is not perfect, perhaps, but it is miraculous.[1]

---

[1] Unfortunately, the genuine original pictures of this period are very rare. The copies, which ingenuous art collectors asked De Chirico to paint, give only a dim reflection of the original ones.

It was not by chance that I mentioned Nietzsche and Schopenhauer in connection with De Chirico. "*A la suite du Nietzsche de L'Ecce Homo, Giorgio de Chirico s'évertua de découvrir le mystère italien*", as Angelo Bardi wrote in *Sélection*, the review André de Ridder published in Antwerp. Schopenhauer is not only the author of an essay, *On Apparitions*. It was from reading him that De Chirico got the idea of the humanness, so to speak, of statues. In one of the first numbers of *Valori Plastici* (April–March, 1919), De Chirico himself wrote: "Schopenhauer advised his fellow countrymen not to place the statues of their famous men on high columns or on pedestals, but on low plinths", as they do in Italy, "where some marble men seem to be on a level with the passers-by and seem to walk beside them".

De Chirico's reaction against Futurist dynamism, as well as the solemn and spectral sense of architecture he inherited from his native Greece and strengthened by getting to know the most metaphysical of Italian cities, eighteenth-century Turin—as well as his own innate leaning towards myth and mystery—goes to explain his expression of his yearning for antiquity. By his origin, culture and inclination, he was destined to rediscover the hereditary sense of antiquity.

But although De Chirico's painting acquired so much prestige ten years later—a prestige without precedent in the history of art—and almost brought about a new humanism and is still surrounded with glory to-day, it was not at first understood in Paris (where De Chirico arrived from Florence in 1911). Not even Apollinaire understood it, though he was certainly aware of it. Of the friendship between the painter of the *Enigma* and the poet of *Alcools* nothing remains except De Chirico's portrait of Apollinaire.[1] Apparently De Chirico's painting was first brought to Apollinaire's notice by Picasso, who, being at that time indifferent to antiquity, only saw his future rival as a *peintre de gares*, rather as Rousseau was looked on as a painter of fortifications. However, two years after his arrival in Paris De Chirico's pictures were bought by Paul Guillaume, who was never a man to miss talent

---

[1] De Chirico painted Apollinaire as a dummy, with his skull pierced by a projectile. A few years later the prophecy of this picture was fulfilled: the soldier-poet was shot in the head during a battle. I knew another example of prophecy in painting. A young Surrealist did a self-portrait, and in the place of one eye he painted a cube with the letter D on it. One night, during a Surrealist celebration, Dom ——, a painter, accidentally caused him to lose that eye.

when pointed out to him. As for the reception the critics gave him, I only need mention Gustave Coquiot's note on De Chirico in his book on *Le Salon des Indépendants*: "Giorgio De Chirico is a visionary who builds lunar architecture and invents titles such as *The Enigma of the Hour, Nostalgia for the Infinite, The Enigma of a Day*, etc. He is rather like Albert Trachsel; curious, interesting—ah! doubtless all this is not banal! But it leaves us indifferent. Trachsel did at least offer certain legends, certain explanations, and his pictures were real lucubrations for madmen."

But Paul Guillaume (the third and the most authoritative of the three Guillaumes who were patrons of modern art) was on the watch, and in 1916 or 1917, in the middle of the war, he got up an artistic-patriotic afternoon party at the *Vieux Colombier* at which he put on show the pictures De Chirico had left behind in Paris when he went to Italy to join up. The exhibition aroused lively interest. The danger threatening the West, to which people at that time were far more intellectually alive than they are to-day, had somehow prepared their minds for De Chirico's metaphysical message. Among the first to respond to it was the poet André Breton, and he gave prestige to De Chirico's work and introduced it to his contemporaries. Later he followed in De Chirico's footsteps and "modernised" ancient mythology. Meanwhile, in Ferrara, De Chirico initiated the Futurist Carrà into metaphysical painting, and imagined he had discovered a young pupil in De Pisis. De Chirico looked back on his Paris exile with bitterness: "All around me the international gang of *modern* painters slogged away stupidly in the midst of their sterile formulas and arid systems. I alone, in my squalid studio in the rue Campagne-Première, began to discern the first ghosts of a more complete, more profound and more complicated art, an art which was—to use a word which I am afraid will give a French critic an attack of diarrhœa—more *metaphysical*.

"New lands appeared on the horizon.

"The huge coloured zinc glove, with its terrible golden finger-nails, swinging over the shop door in the sad wind blowing on city afternoons, revealed to me, with its index pointing down at the flagstones of the pavement, the hidden signs of a new melancholy.

79

"In the centre of a barber's shop window, a cardboard skull, cut out of the strident heroism of dark prehistory, burnt my heart and brain like a recurring song.

"The demons of the city opened the streets to me.

"When I returned home other prophetic phantoms came to meet me.

"I perceived a new sign of the Zodiac on the ceiling as I watched its desperate flight dying out at the other end of the room in the rectangular alcove of the window which opened out on to the mystery of the street.

"The hall door ajar on to the night had the sepulchral solemnity of the stone rolled away from the empty tomb of the man who had arisen. And new prophetic pictures loomed up.

"Like autumn fruits, we are now ready for the new metaphysics."

So metaphysical painting was born, not in Ferrara,[1] as is generally claimed in Italy, but in a sordid studio of the rue Campagne-Première in Montparnasse. That metaphysical painting is fundamentally Italian can hardly be denied from an intellectual point of view, and it has never been questioned by the French. But the fact that it was born in Paris is significant. If it had been imported directly from Italy, it would doubtless have failed to sink its roots into the hearts of French poets. Moreover, Italian or not, it left Italians completely indifferent until it had the approval of Paris.

In the opinion of Giorgio Castelfranco, who, whatever his failings

---

[1] In metaphysical painting Carrà (born at Quargento, province of Alessandria, on February 11, 1881) underlined irony, the third of Savinio's desiderata (De Chirico's irony is more poetic than plastic). Carrà's *Solitude* (in the Giedon Collection, Zurich) is the remains of a man who has undergone every possible amputation—*l'homme tronc*, as the French say—and the artificial parts are inserted into the natural parts. In *The Oval of Apparitions*, an archaic statue of Carrà's childhood holds the tennis racket and ball of the artist's *petite amie*. *Penelope* can open and close like a visor. Carrà's irony would have interested the Surrealists, but they did not know about him. They would never have come across De Chirico had they not seen his works in Paul Guillaume's back room. Actually, Carrà's metaphysical painting has no mystery. It is painting on a human—no longer the divine—plane.

His friendship with De Chirico, their life together in Ferrara—in fact, the whole metaphysical period—were exceedingly profitable to Carrà. It was a straight path which led from *The Oval of Apparitions* to *The Daughter of the West* (1919) and *The Builder's Son* (exhibited for the first time in April, 1921), to *The Pine-tree* (Casella Collection) and the clear seascapes—the *Port of Camogli* (1923) and *After Sunset* and *Sea Morning* (1927). Carrà recovered his *instinct* for painting at Ferrara rather than all those things he claims to have discovered in *Pittura Metafisica*. As long as his instinct did not abandon him, his work remained free from conventionality. It was authentically classical, although I don't think it is quite appropriate to mention the names of Giotto and Massaccio. Carrà is not a Primitive. As we have seen, he contributed irony to metaphysical painting, and irony is not a Primitive characteristic. Carrà revealed what he really was—namely, a *belated realist*—only in 1930. To-day he loves Courbet, Théodore Rousseau, Serafino da Tivoli more than Giotto and Massaccio.

about Matisse, studied De Chirico's work with love, and was one of his first and most faithful collectors, De Chirico owes something to Cubism "at least the inspiration of his colour composition which, towards 1913, does indeed become freer, more rhythmical and more buoyant". But Cubism gave him more than this. His dummies would have been inconceivable without the previous experience of Cubism.

Moreover, De Chirico's work done in this early Paris period expressed his feeling for antiquity on the highest level. In *Memories of Italy*, of the former Gaffé Collection, and in many another picture of the period, De Chirico's perspectives of lunar landscapes have the majestic sonority of a concerto. But, as he himself pointed out, he has nothing in common with a sort of architectonic Wagnerianism: "We who are familiar with the symbols of the metaphysical alphabet know what joys and sorrows are contained in the arch of a portico, in the angle of a street, or in a room, or within the sides of a box. . . ."

As Otto Weininger had already pointed out: "The arc of a circle has an ornamental beauty: it does not signify perfect completion which cannot be discussed like the Midgard circle which surrounds the world, for example. An arc is capable of being completed, it allows room for presentiment." This idea explained to De Chirico why porticoes and arched openings in general had always made an eminently metaphysical impression upon him. But it is important to add that De Chirico's interpretation of it was very different from the sort of interpretation Salvador Dali would have given it. De Chirico's relationship to Surrealism is comparable to Cézanne's relationship to Cubism, but he is not a Surrealist—any more than Cézanne, even if he had lived a few years longer, would have been a Cubist. In fact, Cézanne would have disapproved of people's hasty interpretations of his work, and he might even have objected to a still-life Picasso painted in 1908—which is dominated by Cézanne's legendary cylinder.

But the Surrealists wanted to turn De Chirico into their prophet at all costs, and they tried to impose their party badge of honour on him in an almost Fascist spirit. De Chirico committed the Machia-vellian error of letting them do as they pleased, partly because he did not understand what the Surrealists were aiming at and partly because the clamour around his name was useful to his work. But nothing solid has ever been built up on ambiguity, and the Surrealists' passion for De Chirico ended miserably in a disgusting scandal.

One more word about De Chirico's arches before abandoning them finally with regret. I must point out that their value was not only metaphysical or poetic; they enabled the artist to distribute surfaces and volumes "minutely and prudently" on his canvas and, by means of the simple geometry of their shadows, to suggest a sense of oppression which later, in the works of the Ferrara period, was to be accentuated by the appearance of squares, triangles and other metaphysical symbols rising up like "mysterious stars" behind every plastic representation.

Savinio has defined metaphysical painting as "the complete representation of spiritual need within plastic limitations—the expressive potentiality of the ghostliness of appearances—irony". During his life in Paris De Chirico, Savinio tells us, "felt compelled to rediscover the basis of formal pictorial transformation for himself—just as the Surrealist painter Mirò did ten years later—and this by going over the whole ground afresh so as to return to spiritual finality—now affirmed in a complete plastic entity." Above all, De Chirico must have been interested in the importance assumed by the object in the work of Cézanne, Matisse and the Cubists. By refusing to allow the object's appearance to seduce them, Cubists "managed to transform it radically and make it present to the spirit and the heart".[1] We have seen how Picasso arrived at monumental art when the experience of the first two stages of Cubism had been exhausted. De Chirico was able to intuit that Cubism would inevitably lead to a monumental spirit, and his *Artichokes* (1913) was the first monumental painting in modern art. But De Chirico realised that to make the object impinge itself on the spirit and the heart (and he, like the Cubists, considered that a work of art could set itself no higher aim), there was no point in representing it in the *totality* of forms registered by the memory. Moreover, although he was not a Cubist, he forestalled the evolution of Léger, for example, by fifteen years. De Chirico distributed objects in space, objects seen in elementary simplicity, as with Léger, so as to prevent them being easily recognisable by memory; and thus he avoided making a subject. Work such as *The Biscuits*, of the former

[1] Christian Zervos, *Cahiers d'Art.*

82

Gaffé Collection, or *Evangelical Still-life* (1918), or the famous summer *Nostalgias* of 1917, bring into full plastic life the *équivalences* Léger only discovered in 1930. This has not entirely escaped the notice of Christian Zervos and Tériade, two of the greatest and the most disinterested critics of French art.

But orthodox painters cannot forgive De Chirico for his so-called repertory of phantasms which were so appreciated by poets and writers and give rise to the ambiguity about his Surrealism. The fact that De Chirico was a great poet as well as painter was harmful to him. His purely plastic prophecies passed unnoticed because the objects he arranged in space (the glove with golden finger-nails, the cardboard skull, the shooting-stall dummies) are presented to the painter's intellect by the poet's heart. So it is not surprising that pictures steeped in poetic emotion—for example, *Memories of Italy*, *The Arrival* (in the Barnes Collection), *The Pensive Dummies* (1915), *The Disquieting Muses*, *Hector's Farewell to Andromache*, *The Return of the Prodigal Son*, etc.—should have been defined as "the paintings of a poet". In De Chirico's compositions the "object" is something of a ghost, except, of course, in prophetic pictures, such as *Evangelical Still-life*. But the object is a mysterious apparition, not a hidden reality, as in the no less enigmatic painting of Picasso. If Picasso is the greatest inventor of forms, of plastic reality, that is, De Chirico is the greatest creator of images, or rather, of hallucinations; at first they were steeped in spectral atmosphere, then, after the romantic period, they became "gentle and mild" in order to assemble the emotional relics of ancient Greece; then came the new dummies of 1925, drunk with thought, and the crazed phantoms of trees, the Parthenon, the city of Thebes, Roman gladiators and those Agamemnon's horses which hung in the drawing-room of the Stendhalian father of the prodigal son. Between his two metaphysical periods, De Chirico wanted to complete his knowledge of the *métier* by studying the works of great masters in the Uffizi. Unfortunately, his best known paintings, those most often reproduced in books and reviews, are the least successful in technical quality. From this period came still-lifes with the exquisite and precious quality of enamels—free from all antiquarian reminiscences with skies which had the troubled luminosity of misty landscapes. I think it is a great pity that this period has not been more carefully noticed by the critics. They pay far too much attention to the *Duels à la* Boecklin and to various other mediæval oddities. As regards the works of his second Parisian period, which the Surrealists consider worthless, I agree with Pierre Courthion that De Chirico, when not a prisoner of his own inventions—even if he falls short of the miracle of *La Via Italiana* (1914)—at least attains an intense plastic expressiveness, and at any rate achieves admirably executed scenes.

Did De Pisis (born at Ferrara in 1896) really have a metaphysical period? De Pisis, who knew Carrà and De Chirico, says he did, and, knowing his touchiness, I should never dare to contradict him, even if it were not so. But I do remember how he used to paint monumental fishes on monochrome beaches, speckled with dots and nervous brush-strokes representing human figures.

When I saw De Pisis again in 1925 he was going through a period of real metaphysical fervour. In his pictures of that time, the object, which had now begun to arouse his interest, was intended to suggest a deeper emotion than the purely plastic one—in other words, an emotion of a psychical nature. But soon he allowed himself to be seduced by other more instinctive appeals. I have already pointed out that De Pisis, who has now at last gained the approval of the bourgeoisie (but who can forget the period when these same bourgeois hesitated to accept a picture of his even as a present?), really derives from the best of Boldini. More fortunate than his fellow countryman, Boldini, De Pisis, who is indifferent to the modern anxiety in painting, has found a way of combining the tradition of Venice with French Impressionism. His work, which he now does exclusively with the tip of the brush—delicate and whimsical—had a period of wonderful sonority towards 1930 and immediately afterwards. There may have been more character in it than style, but what an original and healthy character it was! He was not afraid to squash his paint directly on to the canvas, and he had a wonderful breadth in those days. I used a great deal of energy in persuading Pierre Colle to organise De Pisis' first large Paris exhibition,[1] and I introduced him to Zwemmer, who

[1] De Pisis had already exhibited in Rome, at Bragaglia's, and in Paris, at Carmine's in the rue de Seine.

arranged a successful exhibition in London. He returned from London, where he spent several months, with a lightened palette (perhaps the influence of Turner or perhaps only the effect of London's milky light?) and with a new clear and delicate brushwork. Paris collectors, unfortunately, hardly noticed this Tintoretto of still-life, though he lived for many years in the shadow of the towers of St.-Sulpice and was admired by both Picasso and Mirò.

In this Paris was obviously the loser, for De Pisis sometimes managed to say more about Paris than even Maurice Utrillo (born, Montmartre, 1883), and although Utrillo has added nothing to the history of contemporary art as written by Zervos, for example, he is a painter of whom Derain could say: "*On peut le discuter, mais on rencontre presque toujours dans ses toiles le miracle.*"

Critics usually graft the work of Massimo Campigli and Mario Tozzi—two Italians who lived in Paris for many years—on to the main trunk of metaphysical art, since what they understand by metaphysical painting is painting inspired, not by nature, but (according to them) by museums.

When Massimo Campigli (born in Florence, 1895) made his début in Paris towards 1925, he was under the influence of the rules of painting laid down by the review, *Esprit Nouveau*, directed by Ozenfant and Jeanneret. His attention was soon attracted and won over by the importance of the object in modern painting. Retrospectively, Campigli underwent all the phases, trends and fluctuations of modern art. He spent sleepless nights over Juan Gris' guitars, Braque's peaches, Picasso's cubes, Matisse's coffee-pots and orange bowls, and Cézanne's apples. All at once he had a revelation: was it not possible that man, in his millennial essence, was like the "object" and only a pretext? Thus arose Campigli's man-object, woman-guitar, woman-vase. De Chirico's dummies are not an adequate comparison: their oval heads are full of tragic humanity. No; Campigli thinks of more remote times, beyond the boundaries of history, when men had round heads made in the image of the earth: "*La terra simili a se gli abitator produce*",[1] as a poet said. Campigli loved the idea of the mummy, the man-object of the necropolis. But I shall let Campigli speak for himself,

[1] "The earth produces inhabitants which resemble it."

for he has done so more admirably than I can. He uses the third person about himself: "We must give Campigli his place in relationship to the spiritual adventures of the Parisian world during these last years. Among the young the need for certainty has been replaced by the craving for the marvellous—the thirst for the unknown, the exotic. The cinema has become daily bread. Everyone is as familiar with the brothels of Shanghai as they are with the innocence of the Pacific Islands. The universe is opened up to every curiosity. Picasso has appropriated Mexico, the Surrealist Soupault has discovered Paolo Uccello. Frazer's *Golden Bough* has become the gospel of the intellectual vanguard. Ancient and distant things have become miraculously closer. Elective affinities bind together strange parents. Campigli's temperament is rich in contrasts. He is human and abstract, mystical and sensual, brutal and tender. He has recognised himself in the abstractionists and in the Romans. One can speak of paternity, of election, search for a country, a basis, a port. A very Italian reaction against surroundings. In this identification Campigli has rediscovered the aspirations of his childhood. The human head: a bald head. And magically real faces, multiform and uniform at once. As exact as anthropomorphic labels, as impersonal as the faces of the dead. Almost the sub-species man. Roman busts become a living reality for Campigli. He sees them in boxes at the Opera, at the Colombes Stadium, at café tables. If there is a touch of irony, it is classical, pagan irony about venerated things."

But Campigli was not content to paint money-box busts and woman-vases; he was not satisfied with his discovery that man is a clay object and that the vase was the first anatomical sculpture of primitive man. He demands that man, at once milli-form and uniform, should have his epic in paint, like the Renaissance tyrant, like the Cubists' guitar. Is there any danger that Campigli will see his canvas as though it were the wall of a monastic cemetery where the bones of the dead, the skeletons, skulls, tibias and femurs are scrupulously arranged according to rigid ornamental rules? No; we shall find nothing funereal about Campigli's paintings. They are fragile human architectures.

At the basis of Campigli's work is the idea of playtime, man's first escape into the world of illusions: it is a game of coloured quoits and bricks. Campigli, who is not a talker, and in this resembles Mirò, has never told me this. But I suddenly realised it one day. It was on the day he was describing the famous horse by Marino exhibited at a recent Biennial Fair in Venice, and he said: "I like it because it reminds me of a big toy!"

The impassibility of the figures populating Mario Tozzi's[1] universe, as Eugenio d'Ors has said, is the passiveness of Eugenio de Castro's Nereide:

> "*. . . Nereide infeliz*
> *Nada ouve nam vedo que se passa em roda. . . .*"[2]

They have the healthy equilibrium of serenity, doubtless, but also the subtle malady of nostalgia. During those years Tozzi felt deeply the influence of De Chirico, a De Chirico whom even Eugenio d'Ors would have understood and praised if the *Muse Inquietanti* (in the Feroldi Collection) had been as corporeal as Tozzi's *Nereide*. Faithful to the teaching of his first master, a village Leonardo, Tozzi succeeded in combining simplicity of drawing with volume and a love of good materials: the results were often happy and sometimes even astounding. I remember some of Tozzi's large compositions in which there was not a single square inch of paint left inert, so to speak, not a single blank spot. Some of his still-lifes have a wonderful mastery of form, and these live on in the hearts of those who had the good fortune to admire them.

A serious illness, and the desire to embark on mural painting, made Tozzi waste several precious years. Now he has returned to the easel, and he seems to want to incorporate himself in the Lombard tradition.

I must also mention Alberto Savinio, the Apollinaire of metaphysical painting. Apparently it was a poem of Savinio's which gave his brother, De Chirico, the idea of inventing dummies.

Towards 1930 Savinio abandoned literature to devote himself to painting. For a moment one hoped for a new and glorious metaphysical cycle. But then came the crisis, and Savinio had to return to Italy.

But Savinio's imaginary people are remembered in René Huyghe's *Histoire de l'Art Contemporain*—those people "who hid their faces in the heads of fabulous beasts", and "flagellated the human species" with their pungent satire.

[1] Born at Fossombrone in 1895.

[2] "*Unhappy Nereide . . .*
She neither hears nor sees what is around her."

At the Gates of the Absolute

IF instead of a short summary of modern French painting I had intended to write a history of modern art, I would now have to speak at length about German Expressionism.

But for our purposes Expressionism is only interesting owing to the part played in it by Kandinsky and Klee. Later on we shall come to the fantastic and proverbial Chagall, for, though he lived longer in France and in Russia than in Germany, he has been adopted, as it were, by German Expressionism. I must explain myself: I do not in the least consider Expressionism "a symptom of a great spiritual error";[1] indeed, I am only too ready to recognise the sincerity of the painters of the Brücke group: Max Pechstein, Kirchner, Schmidt-Rottluff, Heckel, Mueller, Nolde, Kandinsky and his friend Franz Marc, who was killed in action during the first world war, Macke and Campendonck. Nor do I find the efforts of the "integral" realists, like George Grosz and Otto Dix, any less sincere. In short, I justly appreciate the works of the painters discovered by Flechtheim, the last great Berlin art-dealer, who died in exile in London, and who had succeeded, towards 1930, in building up a certain fame for Max Beckmann and Carl Hofer.

While the French, from Delacroix onwards, had been concerned with giving a new style and meaning to art, the Germans sacrificed style in their endeavour to express a new meaning. If I may venture to twist Cézanne's famous maxim, I should say they wanted to *refaire la nature*, not on Poussin, but on Van Gogh, Cézanne and subsequently on Matisse and Picasso. For, in renouncing *l'art pour l'art* so dear to the French, and in endeavouring to give a new meaning to an art which was still tied, if only by one string, to nature, they obviously had to begin by giving a new meaning to nature. While Kandinsky and Klee, as later the abstract painters and Constructivists, thought that to give a new meaning to art it was necessary to make a break with nature, and Kandinsky did so approximately at the same time as the French Cubists, but with far greater determination.

[1] Corrado Pavolini, *op. cit.*

If it were not for Kandinsky and Klee, I should not be speaking about German art in this book. My impression is that Germany has not produced even the shadow of a painter during recent centuries, although she has unfortunately given the world great leaders and philosophers (I use the word "unfortunately" about philosophers also, as their enormous activity in thought generated a terrifying collective aberration). Kandinsky was a Russian, and the only German thing about him was his scientific puritanism, which he inherited from his maternal grandmother. Klee was obviously German, but he had French refinement in his blood. The same sterility is to be found in Italy as in Germany, for during the Risorgimento—a century of revival, not only in the national and political fields, but in literature and science—Italy made no contribution whatsoever to the plastic arts. The Expressionist-realists of the *Brücke* group rebelled against merely external art and tried to express their intensest emotions, but these were unspeakably timorous and more social and political in character than artistic. Kokoschka alone managed to express himself plastically, though he was not to prove himself as great an artist as Soutine, the Lithuanian of the *Ecole de Paris*, fifteen years later. Indeed, Realist-Expressionism seemed to want to convince the spectator of the horribleness of human nature by accentuating the dramatic element of Van Gogh and Cézanne's distortions, and carrying both these elements to their extreme limits for aims which were realistic rather than artistic. And that is how Realist-Expressionism "re-creates nature on Van Gogh and Cézanne".

Vassili Kandinsky was born on December 4, 1866, in Moscow, and there he studied law and economics. Law has given three great painters to art: Cézanne, Matisse and Kandinsky. Unfortunately, Kandinsky left the discipline of legal studies for painting only in 1897. He took art up seriously in Munich, first at the *Abetzschule* and then at the Academy under von Stuck. By this time Matisse, his junior by a year or so, had already painted *La Desserte* (Freudenbourg Collection) and was looked on as a mature artist, if not a master. "The years from 1903 to 1906 were years of travel. Kandinsky left the closed circle of student life so as to discover new horizons, to receive new impressions and to undergo new emotional experiences. He lived in Tunis, in

Italy and in France. In 1907 he tried his luck in Berlin. In 1908 he returned to Munich, and for four years he was president of the new association for artists there."[1] One night, in 1910, Kandinsky "returned home tired to his studio. The twilight gently confused all outlines and dissolved them into gamuts of blended shades. He was struck by a picture which appealed to his artistic mood. He went closer up to see it better and discovered it was standing upside down on the easel. Therefore what had produced the emotional impression on his spirit was not the artistic treatment of the picture, but just the pure symphony of colours, forms and lines, which had impinged upon his vision and had no link whatsoever with reality. For Kandinsky this was a revelation. He had found his way."[2]

Possibly Kandinsky had not yet read Baudelaire, who had written, fifty years earlier, that a "good way to find out whether a picture is melodious (in colour, melody is the unity or the general colour) is to look at it from such a distance as to make it impossible to distinguish either the subject or the lines. If it is melodious it already has a significance and has already taken its place in the repertory of memories." Of course, it would be childish to suppose it was the melody of that upside-down picture which suggested to Kandinsky the idea of using another art, music, to discover "how it proceeds according to its own methods". Kandinsky, like the Cubists, found no joy in imitating nature, and even wanted to go beyond the Cubists; he had been jealously aware for some years that music, the most immaterial of the arts, could express itself completely without using external forms. What Kandinsky had experienced was more than a revelation: it was a warning. The artist who did not wish to paint landscapes, portraits or still-lifes had to be careful that the non-imitative forms he intended to use to give plastic expression to his own inward world should not be the result of imitations of chance forms.

It did not escape Kandinsky that if, in the use of forms, "music can achieve results impossible in painting, music is inferior to painting with regard to other qualities. For example, music has time at its

---

[1] This is what G. A. Colonna wrote in the Introduction to *Of Spirituality in Art* (Italian edition), and he probably got the information from Will Grohmann's monograph.
[2] G. A. Colonna, *op. cit.*

disposal, and the development of time. Painting, on the other hand, lacks this advantage, but can place before the spectator, in one moment, the entire contents of the work, a thing impossible in music. However, these differences, like everything else in this world, must be understood in a relative sense."

Kandinsky was also aware of attempts made during those years to express a melody in colour. Rimbaud's famous "*A noir, E blanche, I rouge, U vert, O bleu . . .*" had suggested to Mme A. Sacharin-Unkowsky, among others, a "special and precise" method of "transcribing music from the colours of nature, of painting the sounds of nature, of *seeing sounds in terms of colours and hearing colours in terms of music*". Moreover, Scriabin had composed a sort of empirical catalogue of the parallels between tonality in music and colour. Henri Rovel had affirmed that the laws of harmony in painting and music are identical.

But Kandinsky, closer to Gauguin than to Cézanne, was not concerned with external analogies. Kandinsky thought that colour "contains in itself a power, little studied as yet, but enormous and able to exercise an influence on the whole human body", and tried to discover what direct influence colour exercises upon the soul: "Colour is the key. The eye is the hammer. The soul is the piano with many chords. The artist is the hand which, by touching this or that key, makes the human soul vibrate in a predetermined way." And therefore he maintained that the basis of inward necessity lay in the harmony resting exclusively upon "the principle of the keys' ability to achieve a certain definite goal in the human soul". It would thus be a mistake to imagine that when, in 1910, Kandinsky abandoned Post-Impressionism to embark with extreme caution upon the adventure of abstract painting, he thought even for a moment of translating musical fantasies into paint. For him music was an example, not an end. Along the path of abstract painting, Kandinsky the artist advanced side by side with Kandinsky the philosopher and theoretician, who was developing, meanwhile, his first theory of plastic harmony. In 1911 he gave the title *A Lyric* to a picture representing a horse straining to escape. We can interpret this picture metaphorically in terms of the "object" abandoning painting and leaving the ground

91

clear for creative invention. *Autumn* (1912) is already an abstract interpretation of autumn. Finally, in 1913, Kandinsky began his "improvisations", with *White Forms*. "The best pictures dating from this period sometimes give the impression of having been created involuntarily and appear to be the realisation of the super-conscious and a new order, as though Kandinsky were only the instrument of these manifestations."[1] They anticipate, in other words, the automatism of the Surrealists, but only on the surface.

Of course, this is only an impression, for, particularly in these works, Kandinsky shows himself far from being a blind instrument of the subconscious. He insists that colour—whose relationship to form, the effects colour produces on form and vice versa, he had carefully defined—should lead him, conjointly with design, to the pictorial counterpoint which would enable him to make painting into a pure art, like music. He succeeded in turning the obscure tendencies of Expressionism into an æsthetic. Kandinsky's researches were brought to an end when the Kaiser decided to make his people fight a war lest they should become too soft and comfortable. But by some miracle Kandinsky managed to cross the frontier into his own country.

The Neo-Plasticism of the Dutch—Mondrian, Théo van Doesburg, and Vantongerloo—is undeniably an offshoot of the experiments of Kandinsky. Kandinsky defined abstract forms as "resembling purely abstract being, which are alive as such, exert influences and act. They are squares, circles, triangles, rhombs, trapezes and the innumerable other forms which become more and more complicated and have no special mathematical terms to designate them". The *néo-plasticiens*, as they were called by the French, never went beyond these elementary forms. They recognised that their derivation was from Cubism, and wished to carry Cubism to the extreme limits of abstraction because the abstract can be expressed, as though mathematically—though without, of course, reaching absolute validity like mathematics—by plastic reality. Mondrian and his friends thought of the divorce between ancient and modern painting as final and absolute. "Whether we want to admit it or not, we can predict by logic that the future will not understand tragic plasticity, just as the adult cannot understand the

[1] G. Marlier in *Selection*.

soul of a child." "The new plastic art", wrote Mondrian in the review, *De Stijl,* edited by Théo van Doesburg, "is an entirely new form of painting which reunites the subjective character of decoration with the subjective character of painting itself." In other words, Mondrian's coloured planes, and those of his friends, only express relations, "the æsthetic equilibrium of the relationships of the new harmony". In this way Piet Mondrian eliminates all the colours of nature, reduces form to the simple line and opposes the three fundamental tones of the solar spectrum—red, yellow and blue—to black, white and grey.

It is easy to guess the kind of criticism the French Cubists levelled at the Dutch. They felt Neo-Plasticism shrank from "the necessary and sufficient conditions of painting". But Ozenfant and Jeanneret, who supported Cubist æsthetics in their review *Esprit Nouveau,* maintained that this restriction to an elementary form (the rectangle) was nothing more than a stammer: "excellent intentions to purify art, but a vocabulary limited to this one proposition: blue square, yellow square, white square, black square, little white square, little or medium, etc. . . . We can try by sober art to attain to purity of expression. But the means we choose should enable us to say something, and something worth saying. Truth is not necessarily extreme. The extreme is often absurdity: Meissonier, Mondrian." "*La vérité est là où elle est.*"

The Russian painter Malevitch was tormented by preoccupations similar to those of Mondrian, and he purified so much that in the end he was left like Balzac's hero, with little more than a surface bereft of all impure shapes. The only positive result of these extremist tendencies is the thirst, among young painters, for something real, for the palpable object. Malevitch's *Suprematism* was followed therefore by Constructivism—also Russian in origin. Tatlin, Lissitzky and Altman believed in the advent of a new order and a clear break with the past. They decided to renounce painting and sculpture altogether, and resolved to turn to "tangible achievement, to technics and industry".[1] "Constructivist Realism", which appeared later, was due to Gabo and Pevsner.

This recalls to mind the path Marcel Duchamp and Picabia followed in France and then in America (it led them to Dadaism, almost a

[1] P. Westein in *Esprit Nouveau.*

parody and a negation of the past), the path along which Picasso and even Severini (in his portrait of Marinetti, the suit of the future academician is glued straight on to the canvas) had taken a few steps. But in Russia, Constructivism lay behind the revolution in theatrical décor which made Moscow theatres supreme in this field over many years.

Constructivism had its influence on Kandinsky too. He abandoned his German friends of the *Blaue Reiter* group, Feininger and Klee, whose abstractions assumed purely racial characteristics.

Kandinsky, like Picasso, felt at a given moment a need to revert to some of his youthful experiments. As Constructivist it was sufficient for Kandinsky to apply the theories which he had already evolved in 1912. In Russia—and in Germany, where he returned in 1921 (he only settled in France after 1930, and obtained French nationality in 1939)—spheres, triangles and countless other geometrical shapes gradually take the place of the wild romantic shapes of the period of "improvisations". The dramatic power of the *White Shapes* of 1913 and the *Two Reds* of 1916 dissolves into the pure lyricism of *Three Tones* (1926) and *Veiled Incandescence* (1928), and so on, from the great compositions of 1937–8 up to his latest work. Bauer, a German, was a great admirer and supporter of Kandinsky's third period, but, although his relationship to Kandinsky can be compared to Braque's relationship to Picasso, Bauer is not the Braque of abstract painting. Many of Kandinsky's and Bauer's pictures are to be found in the rooms of the Guggenheim Foundation in New York, but there are also others by Kandinsky in the main galleries of America, Japan and Europe, with the exception, of course, of Italy and Spain, which are too hemmed in by antiquarian provincialism.

The pictures dating from Kandinsky's Constructivist period are very open to debate. But I hold with Will Grohmann, Kandinsky's most authoritative critic, who finds they express great serenity, "but a greater inward tension and an increasing wealth of colour and form. . . . He [Kandinsky] has expressed with ever-growing acuteness and precision the irrationalism of his experience, and every indecision has vanished before clarity. All the media of expression are linked together and fused into one. Our eyes must again learn to contemplate polyphonic vision, just as our ears have to grow accustomed to polyphonic listening. A cosmos limited in every sense, but which, by moving in all directions, comes towards us. We feel its importance more than we understand it".

Kandinsky could apply to himself Brancusi's saying: "Do not look for obscure and mysterious formulas. It is pure joy that I give you. Look at them until you can no longer see them. Those who are closest to the Lord have seen them."

But, being more modest, Kandinsky was content to write for my review, *XXème Siècle*: "Don't deceive yourselves. Don't imagine you will *receive* painting only through your eyes. No; you will receive it through your five senses. What is meant by *form* in painting is not only colour. What is known as *design* is another inevitable part of the means of pictorial expression. And, starting from the *dot*, which is at the basis of all other shapes, infinite in number—this little dot is a living being with a huge power over the spirit of man. If the artist places it properly on the canvas, the little dot is satisfied, and it pleases the spectator. It says: Yes, this is me. Do you hear my little sound which is necessary in the great *chorus* of the work? . . . It will never be possible to paint without *colours* and *design*, but painting without the *object* has existed for more than twenty-five years. One may, or one may not, introduce the object into a picture. When I think of all the discussions going on about this *dot*, discussions which started about thirty years ago and have not yet come to an end, I realise the immense strength of painting often called *abstract* or *non-figurative*, though I prefer to call it *concrete*. It raises a *problem* people were too anxious to *bury* hurriedly, a problem said to have been solved once and for all (naturally, in a negative sense), one that doesn't allow itself to be buried. *Concrete* art is in full development in the free countries, and the number of painters who are in favour of the movement grows day by day."[1]

In the United States alone there were about forty such painters, according to a booklet I received in Paris on the eve of the late war. Five of them, Bidermann, Ferren, Gallatin, Morris and Shaw, had already exhibited together a few years earlier, in Paris, at the *Galerie Pierre*, and Zervos had observed that particularly the first two had

[1] Kandinsky died in Paris during the winter of 1945.

"a will straining towards a great destiny". There were also some European abstract painters in America, among others the Germans Feininger, Albers and Moholi-Nagi, and the Frenchman Hélion, who has done some strong and living plastic work. In Paris, towards 1935, the *Abstraction-Création* group gathered round Herbin, Mondrian and Vantongerloo and it was joined by Arp, the good Sophie Tauber, Kurt Seligmann who was about to become a convert to Surrealism, Gorin, the Australian, Power, and the Italians, Enrico Prampolini and Alberto Magnelli. Prampolini, who persisted in believing in Futurism though by now it had lost some of its *raison d'être* owing to the separation from the Divisionists, painted his best pictures during this period. From July 26 to October 21, 1937, the *Musée du Jeu de Paume* devoted a vast exhibition to the origins of contemporary international art and two rooms were consecrated to abstract or non-figurative painters. In Belgium Servranckx formed a Neoplastic group. In England Ben Nicholson has succeeded in expressing a kind of lyrical wonder "through a rational absoluteness of tones and lines as sharp as a razor's edge". And after Kandinsky's death, abstract painting gathered new strength in France too. Artists are coming more and more to admire, not only Pevsner's amazing metal constructions and Arp's pure forms, but also the work of Delaunay, a painter somewhat forgotten during the last few years, and Alberto Magnelli, who is becoming increasingly free.

In July, 1945, the Drouin gallery in Paris got up a large exhibition of concrete art at which were exposed works by Arp, the Delaunays (Robert and Sonia), Domela, Freundlich, Gorin, Herbin, Kandinsky, Magnelli, Mondrian, Pevsner, Tauber-Arp and Van Doesburg. Arp wrote in the catalogue that: "A picture or a work of sculpture without an object as model is every bit as concrete and sensuous as a leaf or a stone." The following year saw the creation of the *Salon des Réalités Nouvelles*—open to non-figurative artists from all over the world.

It might have seemed as if Kandinsky had exhausted all the possibilities of abstract art. But the exhibitions at the Drouin Gallery and at the *Salon des Réalités Nouvelles* have demonstrated the importance of the achievement of Alberto Magnelli (born in Florence in 1888). Magnelli is now certainly the greatest of "concrete" painters after

Kandinsky. (The expression "concrete art" was first adopted, unless I am mistaken, by the Dutch painter Van Doesburg.)

In the words of Leon Degand: "What strikes me immediately in Magnelli's work is his clear decided and terse way of expressing himself. Magnelli's style derives from the perfect adaptation of the form of expression to what needs to be expressed. Magnelli is perhaps the only living artist who shares with Picasso a kind of brutal courage and a complete lack of concessions and politenesses—though his is a domain quite different from and even foreign to Picasso's." For myself I would add that Magnelli has restored to abstract art, after Kandinsky's closed lyricism, its purest monumental spirit. And Degand's comparison with Picasso expresses precisely Magnelli's position at the core of figurative art to-day.

The work of Paul Klee (who died in Switzerland a few years ago, towards his seventieth year) seems, as Roger Vitrac pointed out, to be the spontaneous *écho optique* of even more abstract researches. Klee is the only *artist* Germany has produced in recent years. Even though he appears to have studied Cypriot idols, both clothed and naked, and the graffito decorations of remotest centuries more than the masters of the Rhine, his work is genuinely German. His imagination and technique recall the incisions on the walls of prehistoric caves. But his symbols are those of modern science: crystals, meteors, atoms and the hundred micro-organisms which constitute the daily booty of the microscope. But even if it were true to say that every progress in science involves corresponding progress in the arts, art and science will never be communicating vases. Moreover, Klee the German was by nature more given to magic than to science. The abstract only attracted him because of its mystery. Pierre Guéguen, who, like Georges Duthuit, allows for jokes in art criticism, used to say that the Cubists whitened Negro art. Like the Surrealists, Paul Klee scraped the white off again, but not, like the Surrealists, so as to discover its black magic—in a certain sense the Surrealists seem to have wanted to discover even Nature's Negro art—but in order to discover, beyond its black magic, "the original demiurgic intelligence, divided and split up into tiny elementary spirits, the little souls of the inanimate".

Klee's painting has been called the work of a poet. But it is also the

97

painting of an exquisite artist, one of the few who have been able to express in plastic terms the ephemeral encounters of sensations. He has succeeded in translating the oscillations of sentiments in the labyrinth of the human heart—such as *naïveté*, love, irony—into plastic vibrations. But he did not organise these emotions of the spirit in the way a Post-Impressionist painter arranged a bunch of flowers in a vase, or set out on a kitchen table the still-life he was about to reproduce. Even the most complex of Klee's compositions *coincide* magically "with the phenomena they express, with the emotions they arouse".[1]

Tériade observed that the principal characteristic of Kandinsky and Klee was musical (the new arrangement, that is, of the plastic universe on a basis of harmony), and they had in common their predilection for the infinitesimal, for the tiniest of elements, the dot. But I should like to point out that whereas Klee endeavoured to be precious in his texture, as though he wanted to be "the Odilon Redon of abstract art", Kandinsky, like Matisse, tried to express himself through pure colour rather than texture. What these two modern Primitives have in common is their *popular* sense of art. Kandinsky's geometrical forms and Klee's graffiti constitute, perhaps involuntarily, something like a *return* to the universal source of art, a return to the earliest artistic manifestations of mankind—of mankind already misguided by wars, but not yet stupefied by the notion of its own importance.

The Surrealists spent a long time pondering over Klee. In the end they refused to annex him. (Their behaviour was the opposite of what it had been when they wrongly annexed many of Picasso's and Braque's pictures.) The abstract painters maintained the same reserve. Between two opposed truths, as the poet says, there cannot be, nor should there be, a happy mean.

[1] Roger Vitrac in *Cahiers d'Art*.

The Crisis

WE have seen how, starting out from Cubism, for which Matisse pointed out the importance of the *object*, "Marcel Duchamp and Picabia carried to extreme limits the attempts already made by Braque, Picasso and Severini to introduce real objects into painting".[1] With his compositions in glass and silver wire, in which colour only served to fill up the blank spaces, Marcel Duchamp, *le dandy génial*, anticipated the experiments of the German *mechanicists*, whose work I did not dwell on because it was resolutely outside the field of painting. Later, in New York, Marcel Duchamp became more and more determined to replace paint with elements taken from science and mechanics. Among other activities, he first did a composition which consisted of a cage filled with little squares of marble, like sugar lumps; then he reverted once more to his ingenious *spirals*, thereby creating what the poet, Georges Hugnet (who wrote the history of Dadaism), called *l'anemic cinéma*. Next, as Gabrielle Buffet told the readers of *XXème Siècle*, Duchamp invented a complicated and perfectly logical mechanism which guaranteed the psychological performance of his personages and thus created his last work, *La Mariée mise à nu par ses Célibataires mêmes*. Picabia used photo-realism, freed it from its utilitarian significance, and forestalled Surrealism by forcing it to assume a new reality dependent only upon his own will and pleasure. In this way, he would turn an electric fan into a portrait of Marie Laurencin, or a lamp into a young girl. An American artist, Man Ray, who was to achieve great fame as a photographer, combined the two tendencies in his *rayographs*—photographs obtained by applying the object directly on to the plate.

We have also seen how a new challenge to painting arose in Zurich with the Dada movement during the First World War.

Determined to defeat Futurism on the battle-ground of scandal, the Dadaists defined Dada as follows: "Dada knows everything. Dada

---

[1] C. Zervos in *Cahiers d'Art*.

despises everything. Dada does not speak. Dada has no *idée fixe*. Dada has no flies on it. The ministry has been overthrown. By what? By Dada. Futurism has died. Of what? Of Dada. Dada sifts everything through a new sieve. Dada is bitterness which mocks at everything which has been done before, everything which is sacred and buried in our language and mind and habits. Dada has said to you: Here is humanity and all the fine follies which have made it happy up to the present progressive era. Dada is never right. . . .''

Dada's systematic scepticism thus led to total negation, and tended, according to the definition in *Larousse*, "to render extremely arbitrary, if not to suppress completely, every relationship between thought and expression". Of the artists of the Zurich group, Arp, Tzara and Max Ernst alone were responsible for bringing Dadaism to Paris; Arp and Tzara during the early months of 1919, and Max Ernst a few years later.

In Paris in the same year (1919), three young writers, Louis Aragon, André Breton and Philippe Soupault, "whose poetic and critical formation placed them between Rimbaud and Ducasse, on the one hand, and between Jarry and Apollinaire, on the other",[1] founded a review they ironically called *Littérature*. Dada's devastating anarchism was naturally destined to win them over, although they were already, in a certain sense, "Surrealists". But the history of Surrealism was fated to be one of ambiguity and scandals, sometimes even disgusting ones, and to end in a terrified flight before the Nazi invasion which Breton and his friends did at least have the lucidity to foresee, though they were unable to do anything about it.

The first Surrealist ambiguity, then, arose with Dada. "In the face of eternity every action is vain", declared Tzara. And Breton went even further: "It is inadmissible", he said, "that a man should leave any trace of his passage upon earth." Georges Ribemont-Dessaignes asked himself: "What is beauty? What is ugliness? What is great, strong, weak? What is Carpentier, Renan, Foch?" And he did not hesitate to reply: "*Connais pas, connais pas, connais pas, connais pas.*" And Paul Eluard (not yet the great poet he became later during the German occupation, which he endured with Georges Hugnet and

[1] G. Hugnet, *"Dada à Paris"*, in *Cahiers d'Art*.

some minor Surrealists, including the timid and lovable Dominguez) confessed: "Beauty and ugliness do not seem necessary to us. We are always much more preoccupied with strength or gracefulness, gentleness or brutality, simplicity or numbers."

The Surrealist ambiguity about Dada was perfectly logical, however, as Marcel Raymond rightly pointed out in *De Baudelaire au Surréalisme*: "One may deplore these inhuman negations, but one must understand that at a given moment, and from a philosophical point of view, they were logical and legitimate." The war had brought about a confusion of the spirit. Moreover, those were the years when Einstein invited people to think that all is relative "to circumstances, to man, and nothing in the world is of any importance". André Gide contributed a fragment of *Les Nouvelles Nourritures* to the review, *Littérature*: "*Table rase. J'ai tout balayé, c'en est fait. Je me dresse nu sur la terre vierge, derrière le ciel à repeupler.*" And again: "*Ah, qui délivrera notre esprit des lourdes chaines de la logique?*" And Paul Valéry, the poet of *La Jeune Parque*, after long years of silence, finally left his ivory tower and proclaimed that "a work of art is always a forgery". Lastly, Picasso told Pierre Reverdy that he wanted to make his mind a blank and to start painting again without remembering all the marvels of the past. With a sense of humour which struck many people as being *boche*, reviews like Tzara's *Dada*, *Littérature*, *391* and Picabia's *Cannibale* expressed post-war scepticism or, better still, the fever of destruction which militarists had finally managed to communicate even to intellectuals. But this attitude was certainly more logical than that of the Futurists, who wanted to do away with all æsthetics and burn down all museums, in order to make room for the æsthetics of Futurism and to replace Giorgiones and Titians by Boccionis and Carràs. Dada's purism aimed at being totalitarian. In *La Peinture au Défi*, Aragon even went as far as to say that "nothing in the world would be altered if painting were abandoned altogether".

Consequently, nothing but negative manifestations can be expected from Dadaist painters. Their work is epitomised in Duchamp's *Gioconda with a Moustache* and Picabia's *Sainte Vierge*—which naturally succeeded in infuriating the *passéistes*—and in the *collages* and occasional paintings (though this is hardly the appropriate word) of Arp, Ernst, and Man

H

Ray. But Dada's task, as we have seen, was to clear the field "so as to be able to start out afresh in any direction". As Hugnet pointed out, Dada was purely negative, and enabled Surrealism to assert itself and to gain time. And indeed in this survey we are only interested in Dada for the *esprits étincelants* it produced and because it gave the Surrealists so much to think about.

All through the centuries the relations between the various arts, above all between poetry and painting, have been constant and uniform, but they have never been so closely tied together as during the last fifty years. The reawakening of science and philosophy, which had been drowsing from time immemorial, forced literature to adapt itself to new spiritual demands. Art at once followed suit. Or as often as not it was the other way round, and poetry anticipated revelations which scientists later found names for. For example, all Freud did was to codify those manifestations of the sub-conscious which had been the poet's concern through all the ages. In view of Rimbaud and Lautréamont, Dada was to be expected, and it was also natural that it should transfer itself from Zurich, where it sprang up fortuitously, to France. Obviously, the public only saw Dada as a group of "demoniacs fired with a longing for publicity, despair and mortal glory".[1] But these ambitions and cravings, "sensibility refined to the point of torture, deep and rebellious abstract idealism, avid and vague mysticism"—in other words, the aims the French cultivated without knowing how to satisfy—were bound to lead, as a great French literary critic pointed out in a recent essay, to a cruel collapse and a terrifying crisis on the day any part of the machinery of civilisation broke down. This crisis was undeniably profitable for poetry. "When one thinks of the number of poets we now have and considers the quality and variety of their work", observed this same critic, "one realises that France has rarely reached such heights of pure poetry (distinct, that is, from oratory, music and drama). Since the seventeenth century we have never produced poetry which is so personal, so vigorous, so masculine and so much our own." Apart from Henry de Montherlant, whose magnificent gifts came direct from nature, all recent French poets whom the world at large admires owe something to Dada.

[1] M. Raymond, *op. cit.*

I am above all anxious to explain why it is precisely the painters who are most despised—or admired not so much out of conviction as out of a minority reaction against the contempt in which they are commonly held—who are the companions of these poets.

Replying to Valéry, who said that "the least erasure violates spontaneity", these poets declared: "Let us therefore choose spontaneity and genuineness, let us proceed all of a piece even if it means that we must give up writing literary works." Breton and Aragon took up the study of psychoanalysis; Breton and Eluard discovered in De Chirico's early paintings that ghostlike quality which Savinio defined as "the true, spiritual and substantial essence of every aspect of reality. To reproduce this essence in all its genuineness is the highest aim of art". They remembered a word uttered by Apollinaire on seeing a picture by Chagall: *surréel*. He had not used it to define any particular quality of Chagall's painting, for instead of *surréel* he might just as well have said "marvellous" or "stupendous". It would be foolish therefore to think that Chagall (born 1887) could be appropriated by the Surrealists; for they could not fail to see that in his pictures Chagall was merely describing the legends of his country, the complicated dreams of the ghetto at Vitebsk.

Chagall's painting belongs to the physical world, even if he was obliged to introduce a disturbing element into his equilibrium in order to capture the stirring legends of his childhood. Chagall tells his dreams, with a good deal of plastic vigour, as the sad and strange realities of everyday life; and the colours he uses are the colours of Russian toys and peasant tapestries. There is nothing spectral or phantasmagoric about his work. In fact, like all modern Russian literature and art, Chagall's painting seems to spring from Gogol. When he first stayed in Paris and made friends with the Cubist poet Cendrars, Chagall thought that he was expressing himself in an almost Cubist way. But in some of his pictures he had unconsciously drawn closer to the German Expressionists, who at once welcomed him as one of themselves. This is what caused Chagall to be taken for an Expressionist. After a long period in Russia (from 1914 to 1923) he dispelled this misconception by taking up, on his return to France, the Post-Impressionist manner in vogue among the painters of the

Ecole de Paris. During this war Chagall was lucky enough to be able, like Léger and the Surrealists, to place the expanse of the ocean between the Nazis and his own lovable and delicate person.

Breton had said: "Let us choose spontaneity." And when in 1924 a manifesto announced the formation of a Surrealist group, it was indeed under the auspices of automatism: "We intend to express the real function of thought through psychiatric automatism either in writing, or orally, or in any other way. We shall have a dictatorship of thought without any control being exercised by reason, and it shall be outside the scope of æsthetics or morality." But the poets left themselves a loop-hole. "We allow for a minimum of direction, generally in the sense of adjustment in poetry", said Breton. And painters too allowed themselves "a minimum of direction", except for Duchamp, who was vain enough (which is rare in an artist) to think that he had nothing more to say and therefore retired into private life. From Dada they passed on to Surrealism, gathering a few new recruits such as Malkine, Tanguy, Masson and Mirò on the way.

The first Surrealist artists drew their inspiration from De Chirico's metaphysical paintings (now they cold-shoulder him and cannot forgive him for abandoning his spectral art in favour of a romanticism they find in bad taste) and from Kandinsky and Klee. The sculptor Arp, and Man Ray, who cannot be called painters, went on making their objects and *collages*. But although the other Surrealists refused to call themselves painters and allowed Aragon to proclaim in their name that "whatever springs from the combination of magic with a denial of reality is essentially ethical" and declared that they would "rediscover human possibilities in spite of and beyond painting", they still used line and colour to express themselves and continued to enclose their canvases in scrupulously chosen frames. In other words, they went on functioning as painters, and this entitles us to look on them as painters. But how are we to judge their work? Herbert Read has admitted that "criticism has not yet invented the necessary vocabulary", and so in what way are we to talk about Surrealism? The way Surrealist poets criticise pictures seems to me quite inadequate. For example, Robert Desnos says that Klee has "lived on Mars. He now lives on the memory of that weird world. How he got there or how he came back, no one knows. Some say that he can teach the blind to paint, others say that he is a Martian himself." Another example is afforded by Benjamin Péret, who merely said, when he was opening an exhibition of Mirò's pictures, that he had met a fat man walking down the Champs Elysées wearing the Légion d'Honneur, and that this man had politely asked him to show him the way to the sardine tree. I find myself unable to use this kind of language. I prefer to get round the difficulty like Hemingway, who said, when he was asked for his opinion about Mirò's *Ferme*, which he bought for the modest sum of 4,000 francs: "No one could look at it and not know it had been painted by a great painter." And every time that he met Mirò, Mirò would say: "I'm still very glad, you know, that you have the *Ferme*."

But Joan Mirò (born in Barcelona, 1893)—the most silent and absentminded of all my friends—deserves more comment than this. Mirò is a genuine painter, one of the rare painters of Surrealism, and he must undoubtedly be judged as a painter rather than as a Surrealist.

It took Mirò nine months to paint *La Ferme*, as many months as it takes a woman, as Hemingway pointed out, to have a baby. And when a fellow has painted *La Ferme* or written *Ulysses* (it is still Hemingway talking), it is not necessary for some Alice B. Toklas or other to write his biography. Anyone who hasn't seen *La Ferme* can't possibly write about Mirò, because he can't know where the artist began or where he is going. Although *La Ferme* is not a Surrealist picture, it would be insane to try to describe it, just as insane as to try to sum up Joyce's masterpiece in a few lines. It is a picture full of mistakes. Léonide Massine said that Mirò's art is almost choreography. In *La Ferme* everything is ready for the great dance which the artist was going to make the animal and vegetable elements of his world perform. They are caught at that moment of pause when the photographer says: "Hold it!" The ballet-dancers pose self-consciously before the camera; the donkey, the hens and cockerels, rabbits and pigeons, the horse tied to the wheel of the well, the snails and little sea dragons, the footprints of a peasant girl on the white path, the spades and watering-cans and above it all a round white moon like a hole in the thick cloth of the sky. But already on the branches of a huge knotted tree the leaves are assembled like flocks of swallows ready to fly away. The ballet is starting.

Above all, in *La Naissance du Monde* (1924–5) *La Ferme* is simplified and schematised; it dissolves into more mellow forms and lights up with colour. Mirò really prefers simpler titles like *La Ferme, Terre Labourée, Maternité*. It was René Gaffé who chose the title, *La Naissance du Monde*: "Mirò has two ways of painting skies: either brown like Spain herself, her mountains, landscapes, villages, churches and *ramblas*, or blue, a savage, insolent electric blue which is alone enough to make a picture vibrate. The sky is never static. His sky has nothing of the over-fed, un-buttoned, stomach-airing bourgeois sky about it; nor anything of a miser's sky, skimped, wretched and calamitous. His is an absolute sky, generous, sumptuous, luxurious, festive and magnificent. And his inviting suns, of the purest vermilion like the lamps which light up at night outside certain hospitable houses, require no comment. Mirò's sun is rarely yellow. For isn't he a Catalan? Yellow is probably not sunny enough for Barcelona. Red is better. Yellow only thunders in Van Gogh's skies. Mirò's suns blast like trumpets. They are despotic, masterful, absolute, all-powerful and supreme. Reds, reds, reds painted with the blood of a newly slain bull. It is because of its scarlet globe that I christened this enormous and beautiful picture, which Mirò had not yet named, *La Naissance du Monde*." Mirò understood graphic symbolism, adopted Kandinsky's and Klee's infinitesimal entities and painted an amazing animated cartoon. I am convinced that Mirò never understood what Surrealism was nor what the Surrealists expected of him. To please them, he too made objects; he once stuck a chaffinch feather on to his canvas; another time he added a few notes of music. But Mirò is no more and no less Surrealist than Walt Disney. There is no automatism, no concern for the sub-conscious in his work. It is above all *alive*, so alive that when we look at a picture for some time we see the little dogs moving their ears and wagging their tails, and the dragonflies joyfully beating their wings. The bright colours, the wild rhythm, the inventiveness and poetic vibration in a picture by Mirò gives the same kind of joy one gets from Walt Disney's animated cartoons. One can't compare him with anything else. After Picasso, Mirò is the most gifted inventor of forms in our time. But whereas Picasso (who was Mirò's first collector) is irresistibly drawn towards monumental art, Mirò is no less irresistibly drawn towards the infinitesimal, "the very smallest". Pierre Guéguen, who studied Mirò for a long time, says that towards 1935 Mirò's world only consisted of "hooks, thorns, darts, needles, barbed wire, curved triangles, mallets, spits, concave lenses and distorting lenses, a world of multicoloured horns. . . ." All these things are instruments of torture, as Guéguen might easily have observed, and therefore if Mirò had been an authentic Surrealist, or even just a realist, his painting would arouse sensations of fear. But owing to his magic and despite his well-known weakness for "crude whites, blood-coloured reds, grim yellows and cruel blacks", these pictures, like *La Ferme*, give one nothing but light-hearted and simple joy.

The "very smallest" also attracted and finally conquered Yves Tanguy, who had vainly attempted earlier on to revive De Chirico's Classicism. Tanguy (born 1900) is an authentic Surrealist. His art has an aquarian ghostliness which cannot leave one indifferent. But he is not a great painter.

Nor is Masson a great painter (at least, he wasn't up to 1939, the year of the Surrealist exodus), in spite of all the efforts of *Cahiers d'Art* and *Minotaure* to persuade us to the contrary. (He was a strange individual. I met him at the opening of an exhibition of model suspended houses designed by the American, Nelson. Picasso was there and said: "But then, to bomb these houses, aeroplanes will have to fly underneath them!") Physically Masson (born 1896) is the most fantastic of the Surrealist painters; artistically, he is no less fantastic. I don't know whether he really followed Robert Desnos' advice and shut his eyes when he drew those intricate lyrical dramas which covered the virginal surfaces of his canvases. In those days Masson was said to possess the nervous sensibility of a Marquis de Sade. The Surrealists had not yet grasped their mistake—namely, that only drawings done by a medium, i.e. *à l'état second*, and the drawings of lunatics can conform with Surrealist orthodoxy, and then only in part. Desnos suggested the following method: The painter should draw with his eyes closed; then, on opening his eyes, he should pick up again, out of the confused skein, the Ariadne thread which would enable him to find out which figures to outline. But this method could not be made into a general system and, despite all its fine qualities, it was anecdotal. (A similar system made it possible for Arp to create hallucinating shapes with cotton thread.) Automatism left Masson with a taste for metamorphosis, questionable pregnancies and ghostly apparitions.

But Max Ernst, who, like Arp, approached Surrealism by way of Dada, seems to me a genuine painter. Of all the Surrealists, he is the only one who in his own way has rediscovered the hallucinations of De Chirico's world. Max Ernst is of German origin, but he went to the United States when war broke out and he hasn't returned to Europe since.

Towards 1930 Surrealist painting could be looked upon as the eccentric proof of the crisis which had overtaken art. At that time Tériade viewed Surrealism as something dead, though fifteen years later he discovered its importance and devoted the first thirteen numbers of *Minotaure* almost exclusively to it. "It was a sincere and heartfelt movement", he wrote in those days, "which naturally bowed before the fierce and tumultuous wind which periodically blows on us from the east to fill us with dreams . . . after its fruitful passage across Russia's mysterious humanity and Germany's musical dynamism"; and he was delighted that it should have stimulated "a deep craving for healthiness and a burning desire for happy youthfulness".

And Surrealism did truly seem to have come to an end. Though he had accepted laurels from the Surrealists, De Chirico refused to follow Breton's advice. Picasso, who now and again flashed like a star across the Surrealist sky, once described how, when he had drawn a perfect head with his eyes shut, he tried to repeat the experiment; but this time he drew something which didn't make sense at first, but later turned out to be the same head, upside down. Even if the Surrealists were not always sufficiently on their guard against Picasso's sense of humour, they did not have too many illusions about his fortuitous adherence to their principles. Even Mirò and Masson showed signs of impatience.

Yet, just when all hope seemed lost, another Spaniard, Salvador Dali (born 1904), came to raise their hearts. He was not yet thirty years old, but he was a born painter. (I guarantee this, for I owned his first landscape, painted when he was five years old.) While still a young man attending classes at a Spanish academy he became a secret convert to Surrealism. This almost cost him his life. His father, thinking that he had given birth to a Velasquez, entertained the wildest illusions about his son's future. One day, on chancing to see what the new Velasquez was painting, he flew into a rage and hired some cut-throats to assassinate him. At the age of twenty-seven, Dali was the ablest painter of his generation and the hungriest for human knowledge. In every field his contribution to Surrealism was considerable—so considerable that one can say that it was Dali who brought Surrealism to maturity and who was its final undoing. He brought it to maturity because before him Surrealism had never succeeded in making progress in any of the directions it had chosen. He was its undoing because, little by little, with his irresistible exhibitionism, he ended by turning it into a fashion. It is the Spaniards' lot to destroy systematically every one of their conquests.

Nourished on French poetry and German philosophy, on Rimbaud and Lautréamont (Isidore Ducasse), on Kant and Freud, Dali chose to sacrifice his gifts as a painter in the interests of Surrealism. Dali purposely adopted the technique De Chirico had used in one of his *Summer Nostalgias* (imitating the coloured posters used for advertising summer resorts)—and developed it to perfection. It is exactly the same technique as was used by the Pre-Raphaelites, and no one pointed out its sordidness more violently than Dali himself. But he recognised and accepted the futility of the work of art whose only function was to provide the beholder with obscure gastronomic and sexual pleasure. Man, like the earth, has two poles: his head and his sexual organs; these communicate through the stomach and intestines. At least, this is how Dali looks on man, the being who inspires his work and for whom Dali covers his canvases with images, using all the punctilious accuracy of detail of a miniature-painter.

Like Lautréamont, the poet who even more than Rimbaud *"prend pour les jeunes d'aujourd'hui l'importance d'un prophète"*,[1] Dali aims at achieving *"une infernale grandeur"*. But he adds something more. Because Dali has an almost perfidious sense of self-criticism, he laughs at his

[1] Yves Denis.

own infernal greatness, whereas Lautréamont, who lacked this sense, really believed in the images of his powerful and extravagant imagination, and did not doubt the poetic existence of his monster, Maldoror, for a single moment. At any rate, anyone who has read even one verse of *Les Chants de Maldoror* does not need to ask what Dali represents. I quote at random:

"Quoiqu'il ne possédat pas un visage humain, il me paraissait beau comme les deux longs filaments tentaculiformes d'un insecte; ou plutôt, comme une inhumation précipitée; ou encore, comme la loi de la reconstitution des organes mutilés; et surtout, comme un liquide éminemment putrescible!"

Dali's seductive personality won over to Surrealism other young painters who had been asking themselves for some time which was most interesting: to paint what they saw from their windows, or to paint the secret obsessions of their souls? He also attracted less mature painters. With Kurt Seligmann, who developed from monochromatic abstract painting into a foppish Surrealism of sombre and be-feathered skeletons, and with the questionable painter, Paalen, the abstract school gravitated *en masse* towards Surrealism. A little encyclopædia of Surrealists even had to be published. For a time a lot of hope was placed in an Italian Pre-Surrealist whom I unfortunately never met, Arturo Martini. Apparently, his hallucinating work somehow attracted the attention of Dali and his friends. Some painters were in two minds as to whether to join the Surrealists—for example, Pierre Roy, a very haughty man, Milena Barilli, who has since been given some recognition in America, Antonio Fornari, Leonor Fini and the Swiss Wulliamy, who painted an hallucinating *Trojan Horse*. As for Leonor Fini, I know that Paul Eluard praised her recent work and that the critic, Florent Fels, who became an art dealer, managed to get the *Côte d'Azur* collectors interested in it.

At the Surrealist exhibitions in New York, London and Paris— which attracted huge crowds like the ones at industrial fairs on account of the originality of their *mise en scène*—two exceptionally talented recruits to Surrealism exhibited: René Magritte and Paul Delvaux, both Belgian. Magritte goes in for *trompe l'œil*, for mysterious objects, bare and concrete, suspended in space. Delvaux seems to have rediscovered the metaphysical stupefaction of De Chirico's early painting. Some time ago Paul Fierens wrote to me from Brussels that "Delvaux's star is rapidly rising on the horizon. He has constructed a universe in which simple elements, figures, landscapes and buildings, predominate more and more over the absurdest mechanism and accessories. . . . I think I am not mistaken in heralding him as the painter of to-morrow."

Unlike all the preceding movements, the Surrealist "revolution" set out to be ethical, not artistic. And so it is naturally more interesting from an ethical point of view than from the æsthetic one, which the painters and poets of the sub-conscious persistently derided and mocked.

Dali's is certainly among the most subtle and disturbing dialectics of our age. He is content to apply to painting the technique of Lautréamont, who describes his monstrous personages in minute detail; he paints the most terrifying scenes of his poem with all the patience of a miniaturist. Dali reveals his genius when he talks of "the new colours of spectral sex appeal", or when he gives a paranoiaco-critical interpretation of the haunting image of the Angelus, or, again, when he examines the spectral Surrealism of the Pre-Raphaelite "eternal feminine"; but when he paints, he is only illustrating Lautréamont. Dali, Surrealism's only true painter, is merely the Gustave Doré of *Les Chants de Maldoror*. Whereas De Chirico, when he painted *La Malinconia, Le Nostalgie Estive* and *Le Muse Inquietanti*, brought a new, original and very strange emotion into painting. What I mean is that De Chirico revealed himself as a poet and not as an illustrator, a creator and not just a maker of images. I always felt a deep sympathy for Surrealism, even from the very start, and I am convinced that "the regions which lie between reality and the enchanted world of the irrational" can supply artists with subjects which are no less interesting than the Post-Impressionists' bunches of flowers and orchards.

Of course, a lot of the hatred which Surrealists stir up in the *rapins* of Montparnasse can be attributed to narrow provincialism; but it is also understandable that their intolerance, their party orthodoxy and their organised brawls should arouse intolerance amongst people who mercifully loathe noisy manifestations.

What I really insist on is that Surrealism has only given one great painter to art. It has certainly produced some *esprits étincelants*, and has stirred up some deep searchings which have unfortunately remained inarticulate. But unless Delvaux has really turned out to be the great painter Paul Fierens is hoping for, it seems to me—and I am sorry to have to say it—that Surrealism only represents a crisis and that we may have to watch for its inevitable development for a long time to come.

Looking Around

AND now we are coming to the end of the survey which has taken us in eight stages from Impressionism to abstract painting and Surrealism. I do not know whether the extremist tendencies of these two recent movements will open a new cycle. I am rather inclined to look upon them as the last phase of the revolution initiated by Delacroix which in due course inevitably came under the influence of French poetry (from Baudelaire to Lautréamont) and German philosophy and science (from Hegel to Freud).

Of all the artists whose work we examined, one in particular symbolises modern painting's dramatic evolution during this first half of the twentieth century, Pablo Picasso. Over and over again Picasso could have let himself be satisfied with his progress and sat back comfortably, *"les pieds au chaud, dans le fauteuil de l'inquiétude moderne"*.[1] But his enormous vitality stopped him from doing it. In centuries to come Picasso's painting will bear witness to the need for escape characteristic of powerful personalities. But it will also prove how inexorable the Spaniards are. In a monograph I once published for him, Eugenio d'Ors said that Picasso must be considered Italian, not Spanish. But here Eugenio d'Ors, though he is a brilliant writer on æsthetics, was utterly mistaken. Even Picasso's versatility is a quality only found among the great Spanish masters, as Maurice Raynal rightly pointed out. Italian painting "is entirely subordinated to the magnificence of technique and does not seek to develop itself in any other way than by perfecting its technique". We have only to compare Picasso's versatility with Severini's or De Chirico's or Carrà's to see how genuinely and jealously Spanish Picasso's versatility is. Another peculiar characteristic of great Spanish masters is their *monstrous familiarity* with the object. "The Spaniard's thirst for truth", wrote José Bergamin, "makes him want to find naked truth, bare of its skin, bare to the bone. In Goya, as in Quevedo, Gracian or Calderon these real and living skeletons are a transparent and *irrational* extravagance,

---

[1] This is what Picasso himself accused André Breton of doing.

113

a *dream of reason* which can generate true monsters. But at the same time, in Goya, as in St. Teresa, Cervantes and Lope de Vega, the *reason for dreaming* populates his world with real monsters and loving phantoms." Goya's human monsters, his incredible Bourbons, have their counterpart in Picasso's abstract monstrosities, which, though not Expressionist in the narrow sense, are full of a tremendous expressive intensity. This may or may not be intentional, but that it is so is unquestionable, and it would be impossible to find such intensity in any French painter. In Italy, where people are less convinced of the need for pure painting (owing to the unfortunate results produced by artists who tried to practise it), *Guernica* and Picasso's other pictures of the same period have had far more influence than in France, where his prestige is unquestionably greater. It is easy to prove that Picasso's need to express himself is due to his Spanish origin. The same need is found in other Spanish artists who have not sought contact with France and who—having failed to obtain the worldly success of Zuloaga or José Maria Sert—still express themselves freely. I need only mention José Guttierrez Solana (born in Madrid in 1886), who disregards all intellectual preoccupations and has never looked beyond the Pyrenees. Unlike Picasso's, which is enclosed in a formal language, even in *Guernica*, Solana's Expressionism belongs to popular tradition.

Now and again this satanic need to express a terrifying inner world reappears in a young Portuguese painter of remarkable talent, Vera da Silva, although she has lived in Paris for many years. Some of her pictures made the great and humble Bonnard sigh and say: "This is how I should like to paint!" It also reappears in the most distinguished painters of Latin America: the Mexican, Diego Rivera, who has forgotten his Parisian and Cubist past and is the greatest fresco worker of the century; the Brazilian, Lazar Segall, who, despite his Germanic formation, found in his adopted country an ideal spiritual climate and a tragic source of Expressionism which enabled him to make his *Pogrom* (1937) one of the most moving poems ever inspired by human suffering.

In Solana's painting one discovers Spain, just as one finds Flanders, as Cassou used to say, in James Ensor. The Impressionist Ensor was indeed the prophet of Expressionism in its wider sense, and not only

114

of that Flemish Expressionism which has given Belgium its best artists during the last twenty-five years. Ensor (born at Ostend on April 13, 1860) was certainly one of the most distinguished figures in the art of his time. De Ridder considers that he was a forerunner of Vuillard, Bonnard, and—on account of his vast sonorities—of Matisse. Ensor, who painted *Ma Chambre Préferée* (1892) and *Les Poissons* (1895), does indeed herald Vuillard, Bonnard and Matisse, but Vuillard's and Bonnard's *intimism* and Matisse's sonority have other sources also, as we saw. Thus it is with the skeletons and phantoms with which Ensor filled his plastic universe: although in one sense they can be said to prophesy Surrealism, in actual fact they don't exceed the limits of *le grotesque populaire* which Ensor loved and captured in *La Mort et les Masques* (1888) and *Les Squelettes Musiciens* (1907).

It is a different matter if one says that "his seascapes herald Permeke, his devils Van den Berghe and some of his laconic portraits De Smet"; in other words, that he is a forerunner of the Flemish Expressionists who have revived contemporary Belgian art.

These artists, and Tytgat, who is the juggler of this group, show no traces of French influence. Whether this is a good or bad thing posterity will have to decide. But I must say that, although I am well accustomed to universal plastic languages and ferociously opposed to all nationalisms, I do not consider Belgian Expressionism to be a dialect even if it is not always as clear a language as Ensor's. Although the desperate effort on the part of Flemish painters to cut themselves off from the rest of the world and to listen to no other voices than those of their own country may appear pointless in the eyes of posterity, I think it deserves our respect; especially as the voices they listen to are genuine ones and not the brawling of academies. If one turns one's back on French art, one is forced to make a choice between Academism and Expressionism.

French influence is more marked in Switzerland, but there painting succumbed to the danger the Belgians were able to avoid. Often the painting of the best Swiss artists seems to have sprung from the brushes of mediocre French painters. Still, there are some nudes by Auberjonois, a friend of the writer Ramuz, which prove that very few French painters understood Cubism as well as he did.

Among the French who never really understood Cubism is Dunoyer de Segonzac (born 1884). He is a delightful illustrator and one of the best etchers of our time, but his reputation as a great painter is entirely unmerited. I do not agree with Raymond Escholier and others, who claim that as a landscape painter Segonzac has enriched French art because he reminds us of Millet and Courbet. One doesn't enrich art unless one adds something to it, and Escholier will never manage to prove that Segonzac has added anything to the work of his models and inspirers. The fact that in 1933 he won the Carnegie Prize for an *Hiver en Provence* means nothing, since painters who are far more mediocre than he is have also won it. As for his reclining nudes, even Escholier has admitted that "people have been able to find fault with this admirable draughtsman for allowing himself to be too readily seduced by the fascination of matter and for drawing human forms which are not always decipherable".

It may sound more surprising if I say that Amedeo Modigliani (born at Leghorn, July 12, 1884) did not fully understand Cubism either. His painting derives almost exclusively from his early enthusiasm for the outstanding events of his time: the discovery of the primitives, Cézanne, Fauvism, Negro art, Cubism. Although Modigliani's work seemed destined to collapse at the first blast of wind, owing to its apparent æstheticism, I was entirely reassured by a wonderful retrospective exhibition recently put together by a Paris art gallery. Modigliani's painting has not only stood up to the gusts of wind; it has weathered the tempests of these last years and probably never appeared more alive, more unquestionably true, than it does to-day. The Paris of the *tabarins* which momentarily excited Picasso and Severini left Modigliani indifferent. He always preferred the simplicity of a lovely white apron to the hypocrisy of ostrich feathers and frothy lace drawers. Sometimes, true enough, he allowed himself to be overcome by a mania for stylisation which is an Italian characteristic. But fortunately these moments were rare. His nudes are the most beautiful and moving ever painted by a modern artist. The engraver Gorvel told me how Modigliani used to obtain that curious and unusual texture of his paint, a sort of granulous and chalky surface: as soon as a picture was finished, he would spread a newspaper on it, rub it over with the palm of his hand, and then whisk it off.

So this was the secret of poor Modigliani's texture—poor unhappy Modigliani, who died in the bloom of youth. We can't say he was a very great artist, but he does stand out amongst the most persuasive figures in the *Ecole de Paris*. The *Ecole* honours him as an unhappy hero—its first martyr, in fact. (Note that the term *Ecole de Paris* only came into usage ten years after Modigliani's death.)

After "Modi", the *Ecole de Paris* painters next venerated Maurice V. Utrillo, Suzanne Valadon's son, who is erroneously thought of as a "Sunday painter", the leader of the so-called "popular masters of reality"—in short an imitator of Rousseau. In fact, Utrillo is a Post-Impressionist who was influenced above all by Pisarro. Between 1910 and 1914 he mixed glue, chalk and sand with his oil-paints and miraculously brought Impressionist landscape painting to its highest expression. He achieved this miracle of his "white period" as much *"par l'âme que le peintre y met"* as by introducing his favourite objects— for example, telegraph poles, factory chimneys, lamp-posts, etc., which he was the first to raise to the dignity of *motifs*. But André Bauchant, Camille Bombois, Louis Vivin, Dominique Peyronnet, Jean Eve and Séraphine de Senlis are true "Sunday painters", and true "popular masters of reality", though this reality is, of course, situated outside time and springs from *"le fond le plus permanent de l'homme"* (R. Huyghe).

It is commonly said that one of the characteristics of the *Ecole de Paris*, whose brief existence was cut short by the German invasion, was the revelation of Jewish painting. The east European artists of Jewish origin (Soutine, Chagall, Kremegne, Kikoine, Epstein, Kisling, Zak, Menkès, Max Band, Feder, Mané-Katz, Kanelba, etc.) may differ, on account of their particular sense of humanity, from east European Catholic and Orthodox painters, such as Larionoff, Gontcharova, Annenkoff, Andreenko, who are more inclined to view art as a purely æsthetic fact, and from painters like Terechkovitch and Jean Pougni, who can now be looked upon as straightforward French Post-Impressionists. But we must not forget that Marcoussis, for example (who was a Polish Jew, like Eugène Zak), and many others who developed under the influence of Picasso and the sculptor Jacques

Lipchitz (also of Polish Jewish origin) are much closer to Larionoff than they are to Soutine, Pascin or Moise Kisling.

Chaim Soutine (born in Lithuania in 1894) was first pointed out to Zborowky, the poorest art dealer in Paris, by Modigliani, for whom the young Lithuanian had conceived the strongest admiration. More than any other contemporary artist, Soutine was obsessed by Cézanne's rule that one should draw as one painted, the exact opposite of what "Modi" used to do. Soutine's terrible distortions are due to this fearful incubus, and therefore they have nothing in common with Expressionism. In *Le Pâtissier de Cagnes*, and above all in *Le Bœuf Ecorché*, in the Grenoble Museum, which has been compared with Rembrandt—it was the latter particularly which caused Soutine to be classed among the *peintres maudits* who have Van Gogh at their head—his work reveals a dramatic quality not without analogy with Van Gogh. But there is this difference: failing to find inspirers in French art other than Cézanne, Soutine looked to the Flemish and Spanish. "This Lithuanian Jew", wrote Raymond Escholier in *La Peinture Française au XXème Siècle*, "brings us close to the great mystical painters of Catholic Spain. We could put it more simply, and say that in many of his works Soutine, averse to the idealism and the decorative sense of classical art, is a painter even unto despair and delirium."[1]

Pascin (the pseudonym of Jules Pincas, born at Widdin in Bulgaria in 1885, who committed suicide in Paris on June 1, 1930) is the most touching figure in the *Ecole de Paris* and one of its leading lights. This delicate painter of adolescents, who had the courage to take his life when he realised that he could not escape from the blind alley into which he had plunged, had a "black" period of his own. It is not at all well known, but was rich in work which could only have been conceived and carried out by a great artist.

Moise Kisling prefers even the crudest and brightest colours straight from the tube to any elaborate mixture. Jacques Coquiot rightly remarked that his pictures "are not always in good taste; but when a pictue by Kisling is a success, it is always an attractive work".

Did the Montparnassian *Ecole de Paris* really endanger French

[1] Soutine died of terror in France during the Nazi occupation.

painting? Two notable critics, Elie Faure and Waldemar George, maintained that it did. "If I can look at this untidy bazaar with optimism
from a world standpoint, I can only view it with pessimism from the
more limited standpoint of contemporary art in France. French painting has been literally swept by an avalanche", wrote Dr. Faure in
L'Amour de l'Art (1931), although a few years earlier he had welcomed
his co-religionist, Soutine, as a new Rembrandt. And in *Formes*,
Waldemar George added: "Is the centrifugal movement of the *Ecole
de Paris* a movement of French propaganda? On the contrary, it seems
to be moving from its axis and to be losing its centre of gravity. France
is spreading an art over which it exercises no control. The success of
this art reflects on France, and France appears in the eyes of the
world as a shining beacon. Should not France repudiate works which
cripple her genius?" The split between the Paris of the French and
cosmopolitan Paris which caused Ramuz to make so many bitter
observations in his *Paris* dates from precisely those years. Waldemar
George very seriously put forward the example of certain young
Russians (like Tchelicheff and the Berman brothers, obviously very
gifted, or Christian Bérard, who "copied everything"[1]), and denied
that there had been any artistic evolution during the last fifty years—
from Cézanne, whom he viewed almost as an idiot, to Picasso. He
quite forgot how much he had contributed to the latter's fame.
Eugenio d'Ors advanced even more absurd theories, with the levity
he puts into everything—in his case this is perhaps more of a quality
than a defect. But the Paris of Picasso, Ramuz, Zervos and Hemingway,
of *Minotaure* and, finally, of *XXème Siècle*, decided to make a stand
and began a struggle which corresponded, in the artistic arena, to
that undertaken in the political field by patriots who still believed in
French greatness. New *Salons* were formed: *The Surindépendents*, and
1941. Finally, as in 1913, art was again freed from the tyranny of
preceding generations. The new exhibitions represented not only the
so-called abstract tendencies with Mondrian, Van Doesburg, Arp and
Sophie Tauber-Arp, Hélion, Herbin, Prampolini, Paule Vézelay and
Léger's pupils, Erik Olson and Otto Carlsund; and the Post-Cubists,
Lurçat and Survage, Serge Ferat and Beaudin; but Severini also, and

[1] Gertrude Stein, *op. cit.*

Campigli with his pupil, Renato Paresce; "the primitive" Bauchant, a disciple of the Douanier Rousseau; and the young painters who, at that time, gave so much grounds for promise, the Spaniards Vinès and Borès, the American Graham, Brignoni, Erni, Lapicque, Penado, Junier, and the *fantaisiste* Valentine Prax. The other camp was composed of the young Traditionalists: Charles Blanc—according to Raymond Escholier, an excellent portrait painter; the group composed of Brianchon, Legueult, Oudot, Holy, Poncelet and Planson, who were sheltered by the tradition of the Le Nains, Corot, and Bonnard; Chastel and Cavaillès; the ex-Cubist Souverbie, "who resolutely took up the tradition of Piero della Francesca's school";[1] Fautrier, and the *"indépendents"* Gromaire and Goerg, both of whom, but especially the former, deserve to be better known. In short, while established artists looked on indifferently, painters had divided themselves up into two large groups, one of which was seriously preoccupied with making new conquests, while the other was no less seriously engaged in defending the achievements of the past. The dispute which sprang up on the barren ground of the *Ecole de Paris* had succeeded in creating two enemy camps, both of which were torn with internal strife.

Unfortunately, this was not the only drama for French artists. Another drama, far more serious from the point of view of the future of art itself, was to follow: that of the young painters. The public and the rich dealers concentrated all their interest on artists of the preceding generation. It was impossible for a young artist to break his way through. It had taken the Surrealist revolution to establish the names of Mirò and Dali. All the others felt themselves condemned almost to total indifference even if they managed to find protection through some art dealer or through the benevolence of a few critics. I have already mentioned that only one artist since 1930 has been able to win the favour of collectors—Jacques Villon, who is now in his sixties.

One wonders if the young painters who were formed under the influence of Picasso, Matisse and Braque, and who reached maturity during the German occupation, will be more fortunate? Immediately after the liberation of France, a period of fervent activity started up

[1] Raymond Escholier, *op. cit.*

with a momentum which revealed unexpected vitality in one of the countries that had suffered most during the war. Although this spurt brought about easy fame for many young painters, there are certain names among them which can be considered to have a definite place in the history of contemporary art: Léon Gischia, Fougeron, Pignon, Estève, Tal Coat and a few others. Although they differ from one another in temperament, all of them express a common preoccupation. They are striving to give a positive conclusion to the experiments of Matisse, Picasso and Braque, and to bring back into daylight all that these three discovered in their studios. Their work shows an effort to conciliate Picasso's Expressionism with the noble decorative taste of Matisse and Braque. After thinking out Fauvism again for himself, Gischia seems now to have achieved his aim with real success in a few paintings of a type I should call "geometrical". Fougeron has a more dramatic sensibility; he is more in the vein of Picasso than of Matisse. The others alternate between one or the other of the two tendencies which have been struggling for supremacy in art through the centuries: decoration and expression. Another fine characteristic of these painters is their refusal to assume, as their proud forerunners did, that theirs is the only freedom. They believe, quite simply, that the age of strong personalities is over. To-day that of "painting" has returned—and this requires work of great humility. Léon Gischia, who took in carefully the lessons of Matisse and Picasso, has not come to a stop with the expressive purity of those compositions of his I have called "geometrical". He has now freed himself from all external influences and now at last seems to have found his own independent road—and rigorous renunciation has brought him to reconsider the problem of space.

Though the Surrealist tendency still finds echoes among gifted young English artists, it has been momentarily abandoned in France. Mirò has not yet returned from Spain, where he took refuge at the time of the German invasion. In the States Dali has shut himself up in the ivory tower of his oil-painting and become the portraitist of rich heiresses. De Chirico has come to a no less miserable end. Although he once vituperated the Surrealists, he has recently adopted their technique and now paints still-lifes and mediæval horsemen.

Fortunately, De Chirico has no influence on young Italian artists. They still look to France—but more keenly now than artists of the Fascist period did, for the latter only wished to be guided by France in matters of taste. During the Fascist period an outstanding exception was Morandi. He seemed to have received from the pious hands of the Douanier Rousseau a bunch of artificial flowers and a humble paraffin lamp—simple elements with which he managed to create a poetic and extremely personal plastic world of his own.

After the collapse of the Milanese groups of the "900", the "Romani" were left at the head of Italian art. Giuseppe Capogrossi represents the moderate tendency, and Renato Guttuso uses a strong European language. Mario Mafai frequently succeeds in giving his local tones a European accent. He is a very sensitive artist. Amongst abstract artists, Turcato and Corpora ought to be mentioned. On the other hand with Guttuso, to whom I have already referred, Afro and many others one feels Picasso's influence.

I should like here to recall Severini's course. After a few years' residence in Italy he recently returned to live and work in France. Severini discovered the *object* during his brief but fertile Cubist period which I have already spoken about; and the object has been and is still his greatest love. Among French artists, Braque alone offers such a rare example of faithfulness to Cubism's finest discovery. But whereas Braque definitely isolated the object from his other preoccupations, in Severini's work it is almost always present. This did not prevent the happy balance between figure and object, achieved, for example, in *Pierrot Musicista* (1924),[1] from gradually evolving more and more towards the guitar. But even a portrait by Severini is above all a display of objects. Matisse obtains atmosphere—and atmosphere is the chief aim of painting—by attributing to figures the form of objects, and vice versa. In *Visages de Matisse*, Pierre Courthion ably pointed out Matisse's woman-vase, vase-woman analogies. Severini does not dare to mortify the human figure, but likes to place it, openly, in its proper place. He does not even allow himself the kind of liberties Matisse takes with the object, and prefers its pleasant and authoritative presence, so to say, even if the role it plays in the composition is

[1] In the Rotterdam Museum.

necessarily subordinated to the role of the figure and to the general harmony of the picture.

The evolution of the object in Severini's painting from 1915 until the present time corresponds exactly to the evolution of the artist himself. Through the object, Severini arrived at objectivity, and not, as is so often wrongly said, at Neo-Classicism. The Montefugoni frescoes of 1922 showed that Severini had nothing in common with the preoccupations of Italian artists at that time. He studied the masters of the fifteenth century, not in order to take lazy refuge in their artifices, but to discover the laws of their art. His influence at that time on the Cubists of the *Effort Moderne,* Metzinger, Herbin and Surelli brought about a necessary epuration, like Picasso's Ingres period, and it was beneficial for this reason, if for no other. Always faithful to his new instinctive objectivity (and overcoming the need to rely on the *Section d'Or*), he was able to abandon prismatic colours and to evolve his own mixture and his own texture, a texture inspired by the epidermic surface of his favourite objects, terracotta vases.

Once back in Italy, he again felt the appeal of pure colours. The memories and aspirations of his youth returned to him once more, though tempered by long years of experience.

Where Severini's artistic experience is concerned, it is obviously impossible to speak of adventures. Any liberties he takes with form are all scrupulously accurate. To create the atmosphere or poetry of a painting, he merely needed to inflict a slight twist to a line, suggest a form, or accentuate a colour. There is no sensuality in Severini's colour. He has rediscovered a freshness of colour which has been forgotten, above all in Italy. Severini's faithfulness to contrasts and oppositions is contrary to the present aspirations of young painters, both in France and in Italy, for the latter now prefer tonal relationships. But it would be absurd to maintain that Severini has a merely decorative colour sense. On the contrary, line and colour, the two elements of form, have rarely been more happily balanced than they are in his work. They spring together in one bound; they speak the same language, alive and loose, no doubt, but always chaste and lovable. It seems to me that Severini's latest period is a happy conclusion of all his past experiments.

123

But is it our business to deplore the present decline of artists such as Derain, De Chirico or Chagall? Would we not do better to recall to mind the achievements of these artists which will survive in people's minds and hearts, achievements which gave great prestige to the first half of our century?

Malraux was certainly right in saying: *"Jamais dans l'histoire, d'une poussée unique, n'avaient surgi des œuvres aussi différentes."*

Working in Silence

AS I pointed out earlier on, one artist above all others personifies the dramatic evolution of painting in the first half of the twentieth century, and he is Picasso.

Picasso's success carries our minds back to the great ages of painting. For all that, I wouldn't take on myself to say that his success, which is almost without precedent in the history of art, is due to his best qualities. I really believe that his defects have been responsible for much of the public admiration he has enjoyed. There is no denying that the success of the earliest Picasso went hand in hand with the pathos of the "blue" and "rose" periods. In its early stages Cubism obviously upset people who admired Picasso's Montmartre *filles* and acrobats—but this sense of disorientation didn't last long. Even in his Cubist pictures people soon recognised a "subject"—if only part of a violin or the moustaches of a bullfighter. His "subject" was the Ariadne's thread Picasso offered to the onlooker to help him to enter the labyrinth of the painter's sensations. From that time onwards the game between artist and public became closer.

The artist sets out problems the public must resolve. Thus arises a real kind of collaboration—and it is more intense than what a drama requires from the spectator. Thanks to Picasso, painting became the real drama of the first half of our century.

So it is thanks to the less developed side of his work that Picasso has been able to interest and even amuse the public—because the public always rejoices when through a maze of lines it suddenly espies the horns of the minotaur. Picasso has taken over the myths of the ancient world. True, he has emptied them of all literary content and reduced these myths to formal symbols—but even so they awaken a heartfelt homesickness. Maybe that happened without the artist's knowledge, for he is inevitably only the first person to see his work. But all the same it happened.

Something rather of the same kind occurred also with Braque and

Matisse. The public has admired them above all for their "taste". A painter like Leger who is inspired by modern poems which haven't got a "sentiment" attached to them in people's minds can't hope for the same success. It will never be possible to separate reason from sentiment in people's minds with great precision.

But that is just what we ought to try to do if we want to understand the most significant and fertile adventures painting has been through in the last fifty years—even allowing for the fact that we have not been playing the part of critics so much as of spectators looking at the work of particular artists and adopting different angles of vision at different times. And so we see that in a period of little less than fifty years painting first of all made a great noise about returning to Nature and then, equally noisily, turned away from it again. While I write these lines, Henri Matisse, who is on his sick-bed, is working to make the first "abstract" stained-glass windows in modern art. As this boldest of all the Fauves put it to me, as though to justify his intrepidity: "*Je pense qu'un vitrail n'est qu'une tapisserie transparente qui laisse passer la lumière.*"

From my point of view, the most important and fertile movements in modern painting in France are Fauvism, Cubism and abstract art. The Fauves set colour free, the Cubists set form free, and abstract art set painters free from the slavery of having to represent an external world.

If Picasso can claim to have begun the greatest revolution in painting since the discovery of perspective in the fifteenth century, Kandinsky deserves credit as being the first artist to liberate himself from the object, the first to express himself solely *par des moyens pictureaux*. And we must not forget that Delaunay, when in 1912 he opened his "Windows" on the new realities of painting, said that "painting purely in colours, colours themselves with their play, their sensitiveness, their rhythms and contrasts, make the bonework of rhythmical developments".

The struggle which began about forty years ago between Cubists and abstract artists still goes on to-day between the Post-Cubists and the upholders of "concrete" art. Picasso and Braque were repelled by the idea of cutting the thread which—to use Ozenfant's lively phrase—still tied Nature to one foot of art. Braque said that if that happened a work of art would seem, so to say, never delivered. But that was an overbold affirmation. If we accepted it we would have to deny that compositions by Kandinsky or Magnelli are works of art—and that is beyond discussion.

Yet in my opinion the abstract painters give too much importance to their faith that they are non-objective artists. I believe that the most important thing about Cubism in its early stages and about abstract painting is not the renunciation of the object—but what followed from this renunciation. What mattered was the new need to reconsider the problem of space and to "block" the work in space according to the new grammar of two-dimensional art. (Many abstract artists need to be told that a painting in three dimensions is necessarily objective even if the object represented doesn't exist in Nature, while painting in a single dimension simply isn't conceivable, and whatever it be imagined to be it can't produce a picture.)

To-day Gischia, who is a rigorous and pure artist, but not an abstract one, has the same problem as Magnelli, the abstract painter. It is the problem Delacroix foresaw (despite the many horrible pictures he was responsible for) when he spoke to Baudelaire of "Those mysterious effects of line and colour which, alas! are only felt by a few adepts: that musical and arabesque part which is everything—and for many people is nothing". Gischia doesn't set out to represent or imitate a fruit. He has assimilated the contributions of the Fauves and the Cubists —and not in vain. For all that his work isn't abstract, yet it is blocked in its space, enclosed in its canvas, it isn't objective but is an object itself as much as the abstract monumental work of Magnelli. Matisse was another enemy, in theory, of abstract art, at least before he started to give abstract form to his stained-glass Apocalypse—didn't he too set before himself the same problem in *Jazz*, when he made use of scissors and coloured paper? It may seem surprising that Picasso, who was the first to propound the problem of space in its Cubist and abstract sense, should have missed it so often. But the truth is that Picasso alternates between work which is only a form of taking notes, even if on a grandiose scale (he considers this *"une façon de tenir un journal"*) and more deeply pondered achievements deriving not from some caprice, but from his genius. The pieces now in the Antibes Museum must be counted among the latter.

Does this mean that every work of art which isn't "blocked" in its space in accord with the rules of the latest expression of the plastic arts is to be condemned? It is enough to say that even though it may be in other ways estimable it is *démodé* and out of touch with the age—like the work of those writers who continued to use Latin when masterpieces had already been written in the vulgar tongue.

And now another question. Paris is a city in which truly modern artists are strongly resisted by the public and where they meet with superficial and hypocritical understanding from their own colleagues. Should Paris still be considered the cradle of contemporary art? You can find more intelligent collectors of pictures in Zürich or London, New York or Milan than in Paris. Now, the collector is just as indispensable to an artist as the reader is to a writer. Furthermore, the language of plastics which was discovered or perfected in Paris is now spoken all over the world, it is now the language of South Americans, Italians, Australians or Englishmen, North Americans or Norwegians. In some ways it would be even a good thing if the world art centre moved to Scotland or Calabria, Brazil or New Zealand. For all that, I can't share the opinion of some of those American gallery directors who prefer the clever imitation of Picasso by some artist in Rome to Gischia or Magnelli. I hold that the latest painting can't be a monologue if only because it is a new language. A great painter may indeed arise in Mexico or Calabria and learn the new language with ease, as happened with Guttuso in Italy. But just as Picasso without Matisse wouldn't be Picasso, so the Mexican or Calabrian painter would run the risk of finding no one to measure himself by, and so fall little by little into a disquieting megalomania (I don't want to imply that this will happen to the real Guttuso).

So, though I believe the period of activity of the great dealers—with whom I began this book and to whom I paid my homage—is over, I still believe in Paris. The great dealers tend by nature to impose great personalities, and when great personalities are lacking they are tempted to make middling ones seem great. I have already suggested that the cycle of great personalities is over. There remains good painting. Writers who don't want to be left behind by painters may invent various Dadas or Surrealisms which are useful for literature but harmful for painting. But they will try in vain to pull painting back if they hold on to the coat of Debuffet, who appears to be the latest genius discovered by Paulhan. It may be that the whole epoch started by Baudelaire—the Apollinaire epoch to which Paul Eluard has given such distinction in the last twenty years—is now over. To-day the directors of art galleries are trying to regain time that has been lost and rehabilitate a profession which fell into a miserable decline in the last fifty years. Let us hope they show the same honesty, intelligence and love as Vollard did when he went to look for Cézanne in the forest of Fontainebleau.

Just as after the great commerce of the Greco-Roman world Byzantine painting was born in the silence of the monasteries, so I believe the silent work of the studios will bring to birth the painting of the atomic era.

Index

INDEX

DELACROIX   *Portrait, 1827*   PARIS, LOUVRE

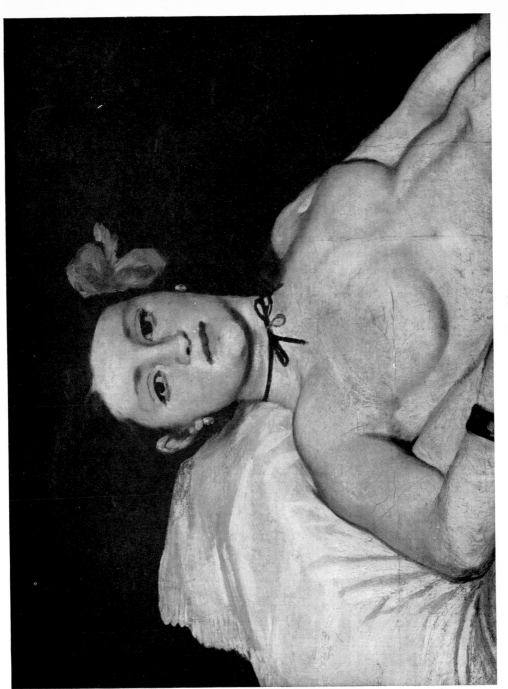

MANET   *Olympia (detail), 1863*

CÉZANNE   *Rocky Landscape, c. 1885–87*   LONDON, TATE GALLERY

CÉZANNE   *Portrait of Madame Cézanne in blue*

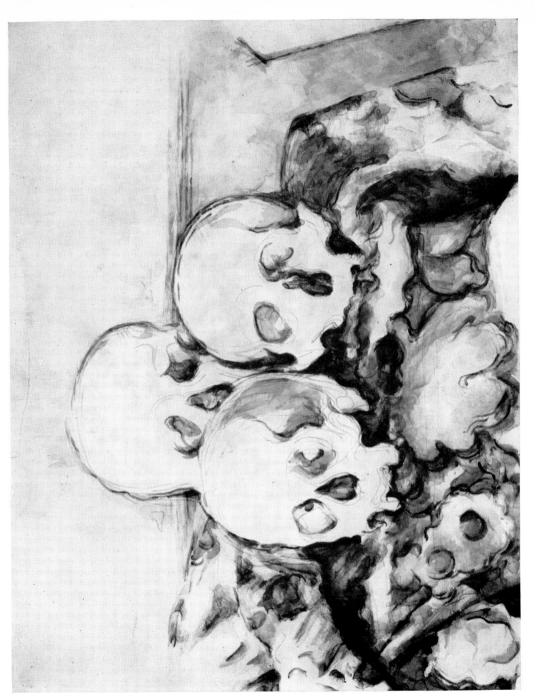

CÉZANNE   *Three Skulls (watercolour)*

RENOIR   *The Plait, 1887*

SEURAT

La baignade, 1883-4

GAUGUIN   *Tahiti Women by the Mango Tree, 1899*

VAN GOGH

Landscape with Cypress Tree, 1889

BONNARD   *The Work Table, 1936*

MATISSE

Woman and Flowers, 1937

MATISSE   *Interior, 1947*   PARIS, PRIVATE COLLECTION

Harvest, 1930

DUFY

PICASSO   *Cubist Abstraction, 1918*

PICASSO   *Negro Sculpture by the Window, 1937*   PRIVATE COLLECTION

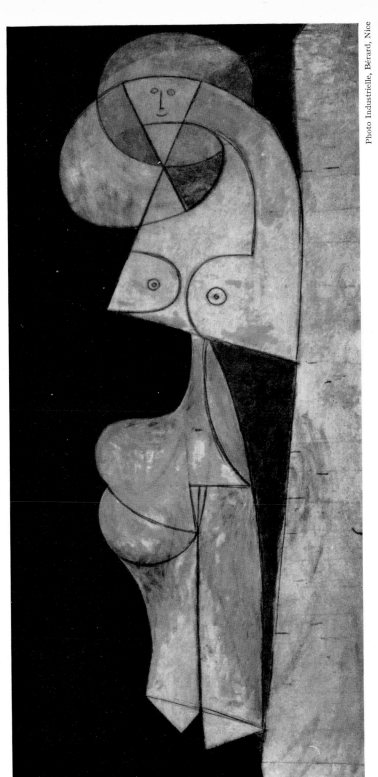

Painting, 1947

PICASSO

La baignade, 1908

DERAIN

BRAQUE   *Boats, 1908*

BRAQUE

Boats, 1948

SEVERINI   *Bal Tabarin, 1913*

Women with Flowers, 1922

LÉGER

GRIS   *Arlequin à table, 1918*

GLEIZES   On Brooklyn Bridge, 1917

ROUSSEAU   *Le rêve, 1910*   NEW YORK, PRIVATE COLLECTION

CHIRICO   *Souvenir d'Italie, 1914*

Photo: Marc Vaux

CAMPIGLI *Le tour de France, 1937*

DE PISIS *Still Life, 1934*

Forme claire, 1913

KANDINSKY

The Little Red Circle, 1944

KANDINSKY

KLEE   *The Strolling Circus, 1937*

DELAUNAY   *Composition, 1945*   NEW YORK, PRIVATE COLLECTION

MAGNELLI

Chemin Coloré, 1947

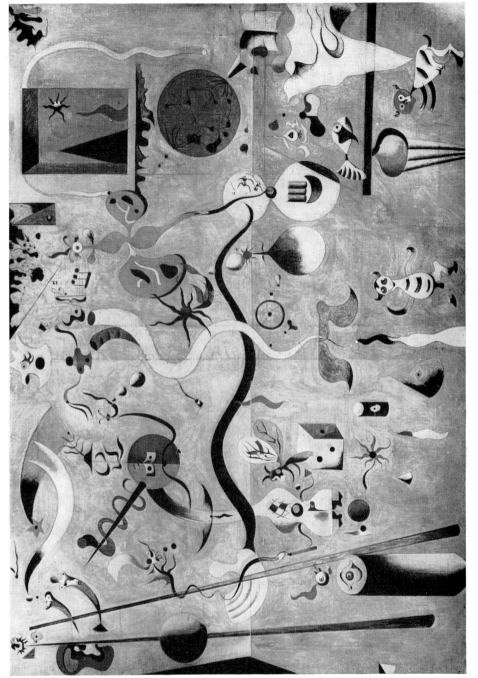

Le carnaval d'Arlequin, 1924

MIRÓ

DALI   *Portrait, 1930*   ROME, PRIVATE COLLECTION

ERNST   *Spanish Dancer*

CHAGALL   *Le poète allongé, 1915*   LONDON, TATE GALLERY

MODIGLIANI   *Portrait of Paul Guillaume, 1915*

SOUTINE   *The Page Boy, 1926*

UTRILLO

Le Moulin de la Galette, c. 1909

Le jeu de courses, 1948

VILLON

PARIS, PRIVATE COLLECTION

Still Life, 1948

GISCHIA

PIGNON

Ostend Boats, 1947

PARIS, PRIVATE COLLECTION